I0799704

studysync®

Reading & Writing Companion

American Literature

UNIT 2

studysync

studysync.com

Send all inquiries to:
BookheadEd Learning, LLC
610 Daniel Young Drive
Sonoma, CA 95476

ISBN 978-1-97-016213-4

5 6 QSX 23

C

Student Guide

Getting Started

Welcome to the StudySync Reading & Writing Companion! In this book, you will find a collection of readings based on the literary focus of the unit you are studying. As you work through the readings, you will be asked to answer questions and perform a variety of tasks designed to help you closely analyze and understand each text selection. Read on for an explanation of each section of this book.

Close Reading and Writing Routine

In each unit, you will read texts and text excerpts that are from or are in some way connected to a particular period of American literature. Each reading encourages a closer look through questions and a short writing assignment.

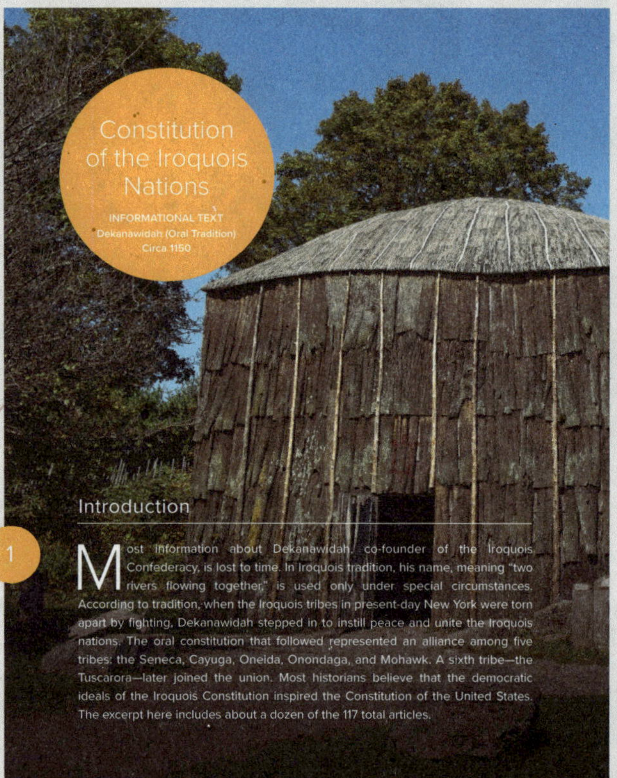

Constitution of the Iroquois Nations

INFORMATIONAL TEXT
Dekanawidah (Oral Tradition)
Circa 1150

1

Introduction

Most information about Dekanawidah, co-founder of the Iroquois Confederacy, is lost to time. In Iroquois tradition, his name, meaning "two rivers flowing together," is used only under special circumstances. According to tradition, when the Iroquois tribes in present-day New York were torn apart by fighting, Dekanawidah stepped in to instill peace and unite the Iroquois nations. The oral constitution that followed represented an alliance among five tribes: the Seneca, Cayuga, Oneida, Onondaga, and Mohawk. A sixth tribe—the Tuscarora—later joined the union. Most historians believe that the democratic ideals of the Iroquois Constitution inspired the Constitution of the United States. The excerpt here includes about a dozen of the 117 total articles.

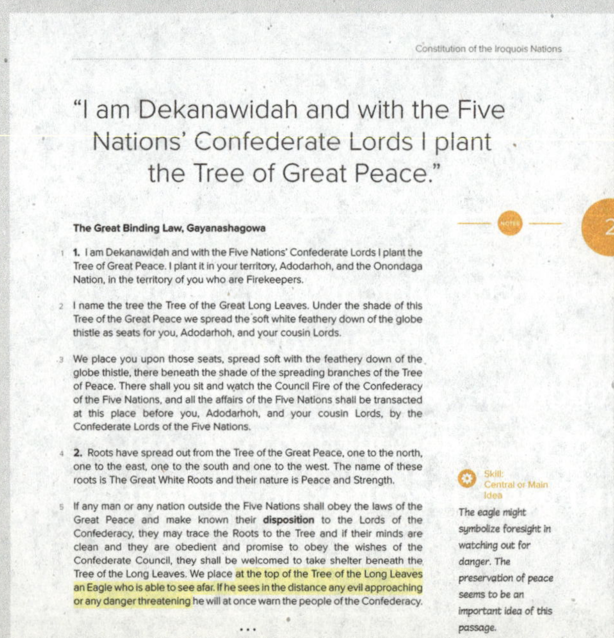

Constitution of the Iroquois Nations

"I am Dekanawidah and with the Five Nations' Confederate Lords I plant the Tree of Great Peace."

The Great Binding Law, Gayanashagowa

NOTES

2

1 **1.** I am Dekanawidah and with the Five Nations' Confederate Lords I plant the Tree of Great Peace. I plant it in your territory, Adodarhoh, and the Onondaga Nation, in the territory of you who are Firekeepers.

2 I name the tree the Tree of the Great Long Leaves. Under the shade of this Tree of the Great Peace we spread the soft white feathery down of the globe thistle as seats for you, Adodarhoh, and your cousin Lords.

3 We place you upon those seats, spread soft with the feathery down of the globe thistle, there beneath the shade of the spreading branches of the Tree of Peace. There shall you sit and watch the Council Fire of the Confederacy of the Five Nations, and all the affairs of the Five Nations shall be transacted at this place before you, Adodarhoh, and your cousin Lords, by the Confederate Lords of the Five Nations.

4 **2.** Roots have spread out from the Tree of the Great Peace, one to the north, one to the east, one to the south and one to the west. The name of these roots is The Great White Roots and their nature is Peace and Strength.

5 If any man or any nation outside the Five Nations shall obey the laws of the Great Peace and make known their **disposition** to the Lords of the Confederacy, they may trace the Roots to the Tree and if their minds are clean and they are obedient and promise to obey the wishes of the Confederate Council, they shall be welcomed to take shelter beneath the Tree of the Long Leaves. We place at the top of the Tree of the Long Leaves an Eagle who is able to see afar. If he sees in the distance any evil approaching or any danger threatening he will at once warn the people of the Confederacy.

...

Skill: Central or Main Idea

The eagle might symbolize foresight in watching out for danger. The preservation of peace seems to be an important idea of this passage.

1 Introduction

An Introduction to each text provides historical context for your reading as well as information about the author. You will also learn about the genre of the text and the year in which it was written.

2 Notes

Many times, while working through the activities after each text, you will be asked to **annotate** or **make annotations** about what you are reading. This means that you should highlight or underline words in the text and use the "Notes" column to make comments or jot down any questions you have. You may also want to note any unfamiliar vocabulary words here.

You will also see sample student annotations to go along with the Skill lesson for that text.

3 First Read

During your first reading of each selection, you should just try to get a general idea of the content and message of the reading. Don't worry if there are parts you don't understand or words that are unfamiliar to you. You'll have an opportunity later to dive deeper into the text.

4 Think Questions

These questions will ask you to start thinking critically about the text, asking specific questions about its purpose, and making connections to your prior knowledge and reading experiences. To answer these questions, you should go back to the text and draw upon specific evidence to support your responses. You will also begin to explore some of the more challenging vocabulary words in the selection.

5 Skills

Each Skill includes two parts: Checklist and Your Turn. In the Checklist, you will learn the process for analyzing the text. The model student annotations in the text provide examples of how you might make your own notes following the instructions in the Checklist. In the Your Turn, you will use those same instructions to practice the skill.

Constitution of the Iroquois Nations

3 

First Read

Read the Constitution of the Iroquois Nations. After you read, complete the Think Questions below.

4 THINK QUESTIONS

1. Do you think that the "Tree of the Great Peace" is real, symbolic, or a combination of both? Support your interpretation with evidence from the text.
2. According to Articles 1 and 10, how did the role of the Onondaga people differ from the roles of the other four tribes of the Iroquois nation? Provide details from the text to support your answer.
3. What does the bundle of arrows in Article 57 symbolize? What does this symbolism suggest is the main purpose of the Iroquois Constitution? Provide details from the text to support your answer.
4. Consider the usage of the word **unanimously** within the text in Article 10. Do you think that the initial letters *un* in *unanimously* refer to the Latin prefix for "one" (as in *unicycle*) or "not" (as in *uncooperative*)? Use evidence from the text to support your answer.
5. Use context to determine the meaning of the word **upbraid** as it is used in the Constitution of the Iroquois Nations. Write your definition of *upbraid* here and explain which context clues helped you determine its meaning.

Constitution of the Iroquois Nations

5 

Skill:
Central or Main Idea

Use the Checklist to analyze Central or Main Idea in the Constitution of the Iroquois Nations. Refer to the sample student annotations about Central or Main Ideas in the text.

••• CHECKLIST FOR CENTRAL OR MAIN IDEA

In order to identify two or more central ideas of a text, note the following:

- ✓ the main idea in each paragraph or group of paragraphs
- ✓ key details in each paragraph or section of text, distinguishing what they have in common
- ✓ whether the details contain information that could indicate more than one main idea in a text
  - a science text, for example, may provide information about a specific environment and also a message on ecological awareness
  - a biography may contain equally important ideas about a person's achievements, influence, and the time period in which the person lives or lived
- ✓ when each central idea emerges
- ✓ ways that the central ideas interact and build on one another

To determine two or more central ideas of a text and analyze their development over the course of the text, including how they interact and build on one another to provide a complex analysis, consider the following questions:

- ✓ What main idea(s) do the details in each paragraph explain or describe?
- ✓ What central or main ideas do all the paragraphs support?
- ✓ How do the central ideas interact and build on one another? How does that affect when they emerge?
- ✓ How might you provide an objective summary of the text? What details would you include?

YOUR TURN

5

1. This question has two parts. First, answer Part A. Then, answer Part B.

Part A: Which of the following central tenets or beliefs of the Five Nations can be inferred from this passage?

- O A. Women had all the political power.
- O B. Women decided who could be leaders.
- O C. Men had all the political power.
- O D. Men decided who could be leaders.

Part B: Which excerpt from the passage best provides evidence to support the answer identified in Part A?

- O A. "If a Lord of the Confederacy should seek to establish any authority independent of the jurisdiction of the Confederacy of the Great Peace, which is the Five Nations . . ."
- O B. ". . . he shall be warned three times in open council, first by the women relatives . . ."
- O C. "If the offending Lord is still obdurate he shall be dismissed by the War Chief . . ."
- O D. "His nation shall then install the candidate nominated by the female name holders of his family."

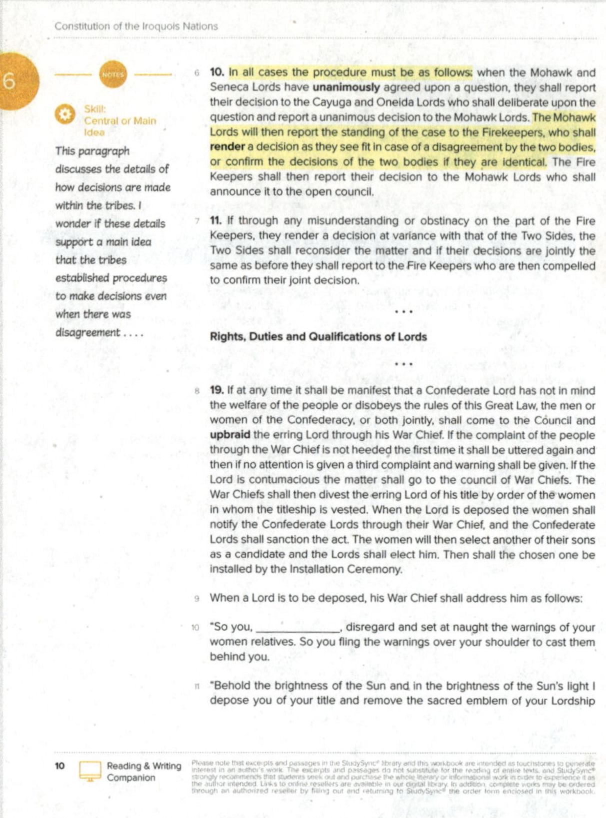

Constitution of the Iroquois Nations

6

NOTES

Skill: Central or Main Idea

This paragraph discusses the details of how decisions are made within the tribes. I wonder if these details support a main idea that the tribes established procedures to make decisions even when there was disagreement . . . .

6 **10.** In all cases the procedure must be as follows: when the Mohawk and Seneca Lords have **unanimously** agreed upon a question, they shall report their decision to the Cayuga and Oneida Lords who shall deliberate upon the question and report a unanimous decision to the Mohawk Lords. The Mohawk Lords will then report the standing of the case to the Firekeepers, who shall **render** a decision as they see fit in case of a disagreement by the two bodies, or confirm the decisions of the two bodies if they are identical. The Fire Keepers shall then report their decision to the Mohawk Lords who shall announce it to the open council.

7 **11.** If through any misunderstanding or obstinacy on the part of the Fire Keepers, they render a decision at variance with that of the Two Sides, the Two Sides shall reconsider the matter and if their decisions are jointly the same as before they shall report to the Fire Keepers who are then compelled to confirm their joint decision.

. . .

Rights, Duties and Qualifications of Lords

. . .

8 **19.** If at any time it shall be manifest that a Confederate Lord has not in mind the welfare of the people or disobeys the rules of this Great Law, the men or women of the Confederacy, or both jointly, shall come to the Council and **upbraid** the erring Lord through his War Chief. If the complaint of the people through the War Chief is not heeded the first time it shall be uttered again and then if no attention is given a third complaint and warning shall be given. If the Lord is contumacious the matter shall go to the council of War Chiefs. The War Chiefs shall then divest the erring Lord of his title by order of the women in whom the titleship is vested. When the Lord is deposed the women shall notify the Confederate Lords through their War Chief, and the Confederate Lords shall sanction the act. The women will then select another of their sons as a candidate and the Lords shall elect him. Then shall the chosen one be installed by the Installation Ceremony.

9 When a Lord is to be deposed, his War Chief shall address him as follows:

10 "So you, __________, disregard and set at naught the warnings of your women relatives. So you fling the warnings over your shoulder to cast them behind you.

11 "Behold the brightness of the Sun and in the brightness of the Sun's light I depose you of your title and remove the sacred emblem of your Lordship

10 Reading & Writing Companion

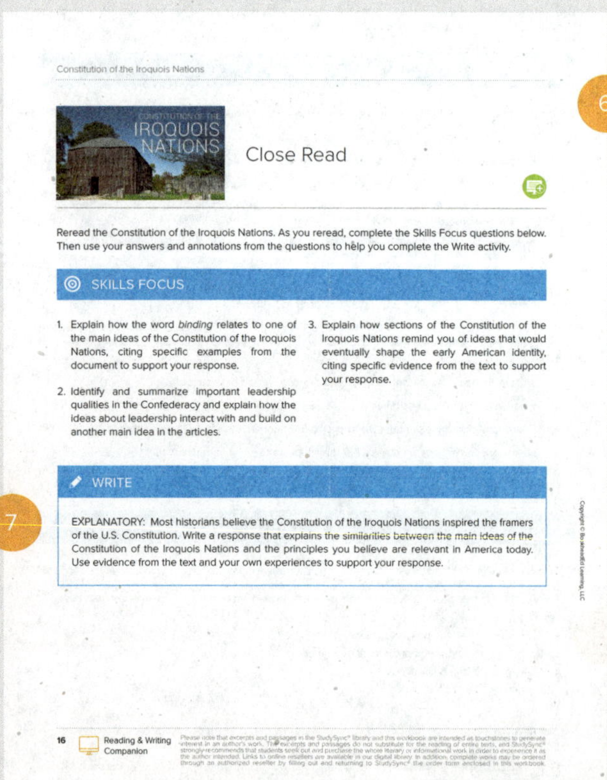

Constitution of the Iroquois Nations

CONSTITUTION OF THE IROQUOIS NATIONS

Close Read

6

Reread the Constitution of the Iroquois Nations. As you reread, complete the Skills Focus questions below. Then use your answers and annotations from the questions to help you complete the Write activity.

SKILLS FOCUS

1. Explain how the word *binding* relates to one of the main ideas of the Constitution of the Iroquois Nations, citing specific examples from the document to support your response.
2. Identify and summarize important leadership qualities in the Confederacy and explain how the ideas about leadership interact with and build on another main idea in the articles.
3. Explain how sections of the Constitution of the Iroquois Nations remind you of ideas that would eventually shape the early American identity, citing specific evidence from the text to support your response.

WRITE

7

EXPLANATORY: Most historians believe the Constitution of the Iroquois Nations inspired the framers of the U.S. Constitution. Write a response that explains the similarities between the main ideas of the Constitution of the Iroquois Nations and the principles you believe are relevant in America today. Use evidence from the text and your own experiences to support your response.

16 Reading & Writing Companion

6 Close Read & Skills Focus

After you have completed the First Read, you will be asked to go back and read the text more closely and critically. Before you begin your Close Read, you should read through the Skills Focus to get an idea of the concepts you will want to focus on during your second reading. You should work through the Skills Focus by making annotations, highlighting important concepts, and writing notes or questions in the "Notes" column. Depending on instructions from your teacher, you may need to respond online or use a separate piece of paper to start expanding on your thoughts and ideas.

7 Write

Your study of each selection will end with a writing assignment. For this assignment, you should use your notes, annotations, personal ideas, and answers to both the Think and the Skills Focus questions. Be sure to read the prompt carefully and address each part of it in your writing.

Extended Writing Project and Grammar

This is your opportunity to use genre characteristics and craft to compose meaningful, longer written works exploring the theme of each unit. You will draw information from your readings, research, and own life experiences to complete the assignment.

1 Writing Project

After you have read all of the unit text selections, you will move on to a writing project. Each project will guide you through the process of writing your essay. Student models will provide guidance and help you organize your thoughts. One unit ends with an **Extended Oral Project,** which will give you an opportunity to develop your oral language and communication skills.

2 Writing Process Steps

There are four steps in the writing process: Plan, Draft, Revise, and Edit and Publish. During each step, you will form and shape your writing project, and each lesson's peer review will give you the chance to receive feedback from your peers and teacher.

3 Writing Skills

Each Skill lesson focuses on a specific strategy or technique that you will use during your writing project. Each lesson presents a process for applying the skill to your own work and gives you the opportunity to practice it to improve your writing.

1

2

3

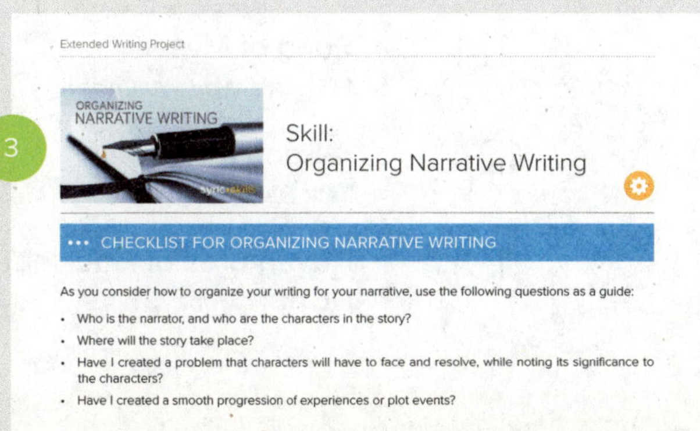

Free and Independent

How do our experiences inform our perspectives?

Literary Focus: TRANSCENDENTALISM AND ROMANTICISM

Texts

Paired Readings

Extended Writing Project and Grammar

Talk Back Text

Talk Back Texts are works from a later period that engage with the themes and tropes of the unit's literary focus. Demonstrating that literature is always in conversation, these texts provide dynamic new perspectives to complement the unit's more traditional chronology.

Unit 2: Free and Independent

How do our experiences inform our perspectives?

EMILY DICKINSON

Author of over 1,100 poems, Emily Dickinson (1830–1886) went virtually unpublished until after her death. Dickinson is recognized now as one of America's greatest poets. Critic Harold Bloom placed her on his list of the twenty-six central writers of Western Civilization. Schools are named after her, from New York City to Bozeman, Montana, and her work has been translated into numerous languages, including French, Spanish, Farsi, Kurdish, and Russian. She died at 55 years old.

RALPH WALDO EMERSON

Transcendentalist essayist, philosopher, and mentor to Thoreau, Ralph Waldo Emerson (1803–1882) was born in Boston, Massachusetts, and would spend most of his life in that state. His work, usually first delivered as lectures and then revised for print, focused on individualism and naturalism, often critiquing elements of society. Widely quoted to this day, Emerson urges us to, "Trust thyself: every heart vibrates to that iron string."

MARGARET FULLER

American journalism's first full-time female book reviewer, Margaret Fuller (1810–1850) grew up in Cambridge, Massachusetts, under the enthusiastic tutelage of her father. Considered at the time one of the best-read people in New England, Fuller's writing focused on reform and ideals of Transcendentalism and early feminism. Fuller was renowned for her quick wit, temper, and outspoken personality, and is even suspected to be in part an inspiration for Hawthorne's Hester Prynne in *The Scarlet Letter.*

ABRAHAM LINCOLN

The 16th president of the United States, the commander in chief of the Union Army during the Civil War, and the first president to be assassinated, Abraham Lincoln (1809–1865) was born in a one-room log cabin on a farm in Kentucky. He served as a captain in the Illinois Militia during the Black Hawk War, as New Salem's postmaster and county surveyor, and was admitted to the Illinois State Bar in 1836. He is best known for preserving the Union, as well as declaring and implementing the legal emancipation of enslaved people in America.

HERMAN MELVILLE

While most rememberd for his novel *Moby-Dick* (1851), Herman Melville (1819–1891) also wrote short stories and poems. "Bartleby the Scrivener: A Story of Wall Street" (1853), now considered to be one of the first great stories of corporate discontent, deploys an absurdist humor—notably, Bartleby's iconic refrain "I would prefer not to"—to reflect on modern American work culture. Melville died in relative obscurity, his work only beginning to receive critical acclaim in the 1920s.

EDGAR ALLAN POE

Edgar Allan Poe (1809–1949) may be best known for his poetry and his short stories, including "The Fall of the House of Usher," but he also wrote a novel. *The Narrative of Arthur Gordon Pym of Nantucket* (1838) tells the story of a young man, Pym, intoxicated by the prospect of the open sea. Pym becomes a stowaway on a whaling ship that suffers a mutiny by its crew and weathers a violent storm. Written as a "found text," one scholar referred to the text as "one of the most elusive major texts of American literature." Poe died at the age of forty.

JOHN ROSS

Chief John Ross (1790–1866), born to a Cherokee mother and a Scottish father, served in a Cherokee regiment during the War of 1812 and negotiated on behalf of his people against the US government, which sought their relocation. In 1828, he was permanently elected principal chief of the Cherokee. Chief Ross's wife was among the nearly 25% of the Cherokee people who perished during the government's infamous Trail of Tears forced march. Chief Ross died in Washington, DC, on a trip to negotiate terms after the Civil War.

LUCY STANTON

Frequently considered the first African American woman to earn a four-year degree, Lucy Stanton (1831–1910) graduated from Oberlin College in Ohio in 1850. As president of the Oberlin Ladies' Literary Society, she was invited to speak at her class's commencement ceremony, where she gave her now-famous speech "A Plea for the Oppressed," just two weeks before the implementation of the Fugitive Slave Act. Stanton was born and raised in Cleveland, Ohio, and after college, she worked as a school principal and married a former classmate, William Howard Day.

HENRY DAVID THOREAU

Henry David Thoreau (1817–1862) was born in Concord, Massachusetts. He is widely known for his work *Walden: or, Life in the Woods,* a memoir detailing his Transcendental reflections on living a simple life in nature and being self-reliant. Of his time there, he wrote, "I went to the woods because I wished to live deliberately." His essay "Civil Disobedience" inspired many key figures years later, including Mahatma Gandhi and Martin Luther King Jr. Thoreau was a lifelong abolitionist and a graduate of Harvard College.

MELVIN B. TOLSON

Denzel Washington portrayed coach, poet, politician, and columnist Melvin Tolson (1898–1966) in the 2007 film *The Great Debaters,* which followed the historically black Wiley College's debate team as they took part in the first interracial collegiate debate in the South. Tolson, from Kansas City, Missouri, graduated from Lincoln University in Pennsylvania and moved to Marshall, Texas, where he taught English and coached debate. As an author, Tolson wrote two plays, published three collections of poetry, and wrote a column for the *Washington Tribune.*

MARK TWAIN

Born Samuel Langhorne Clemens (1835–1910) and raised in Hannibal, Missouri, the author is best known as Mark Twain. His childhood growing up along the Mississippi River inspired his most famous works including *The Adventures of Tom Sawyer* and *Adventures of Huckleberry Finn*. He dreamed of being a steamboat captain and eventually piloted ships down the Mississippi, an experience that inspired his pen name. He was born under Halley's Comet in 1835 and predicted he'd die when it returned. He did, in 1910, one day after the comet's closest approach to Earth.

WALT WHITMAN

At the age of four, Walt Whitman (1819–1892) and his family moved to Brooklyn, New York; by the age of eleven, his father took him out of school and got him a job working in an office. At seventeen, he began working as a teacher, and two years later, he started his own weekly paper. By twenty-seven, he edited the *Brooklyn Daily Eagle* and a decade later, he paid to publish the first edition of *Leaves of Grass* himself. Though praised by Ralph Waldo Emerson, it was initially criticized for its potentially offensive content.

LITERARY FOCUS: Transcendentalism and Romanticism

Introduction

This informational text provides readers with insight into the history and culture behind the Romantic and Transcendentalist movements, offering a portrait of the society and social climate that gave rise to some of the most well-respected authors of American literature. In a society increasingly dominated by industrialism, these literary and philosophical movements rebelliously celebrated nature and the individual. This text demonstrates how Romantic and Transcendentalist writers provided a strong, inspiring new literary foundation for an America that was attempting to show the world just who and what it was. Soon, Henry David Thoreau had breathed fresh life into the essay, and Walt Whitman pioneered a new form of poetry that would come to be the preferred form for great poets from Emily Dickinson to Nikki Giovanni.

"According to Emerson, the highest form of language was the language of nature."

NOTES

1 When you think of the word **Romanticism**, what movies come to mind? *Titanic*, perhaps? *Love & Basketball*? *The Notebook* or *The Fault in Our Stars*? You wouldn't be wrong to think that Romanticism has a lot to do with emotion. But you might be surprised to learn that movies like *Star Wars: Rogue One*, Wes Anderson's *Moonrise Kingdom*, *Princess Mononoke*, and the independent film *Captain Fantastic* exemplify the qualities of "big R" Romanticism more than the "little r" romance movies that may have first come to mind. It's true that *Titanic* has some elements of Romanticism and romance, and the same goes for *Moonrise Kingdom*. So how can we differentiate Romanticism from romanticism?

Romanticism

2 "Big R" Romanticism—as opposed to "little r" romanticism—dealt with big emotions and ideas. Beginning in the late eighteenth century in Europe, Romanticism was a philosophical, artistic, and literary movement that developed partly as a reaction to the Enlightenment. Romantics prized individualism and rejected rapidly expanding **industrialism** in favor of a renewed reverence for nature. Romantic artists and poets often regarded the formalism—adherence to traditional structures and forms—of the Enlightenment as confining and artificial. European Romantic authors included Stendhal, Goethe, Lord Byron, Coleridge, Wordsworth, and Mary Shelley.

The Oxbow (The Connecticut River at Northampton) by Thomas Cole

NOTES

3 When Romantic ideals reached America in the early nineteenth century, the nation was caught up in a massive westward expansion and was simultaneously trying to define what it was to be American, both to itself and to the world. As American cities and towns grew, people had more time for philosophical and creative endeavors and began to write original works of fiction and poetry, as well as contemplative essays. Spanning from 1820 until the end of the Civil War in 1865, American Romanticism was highly concerned with the individual and this was reflected in the literature of the era. American Romantics placed a high value on nature, seeing it as something that brought one closer to one's true self. Renouncing blind obedience to the customs of the past, American artists and writers of the period embraced emotion, imagination, liberation, free expression, and a fascination with mysticism and the supernatural. American Romantic authors included Washington Irving, James Fenimore Cooper, Nathaniel Hawthorne, Herman Melville, Walt Whitman, and Edgar Allan Poe. American Romanticism made the world sit up and take notice of American literature.

Transcendentalism

4 **Transcendentalism** developed in the lates 1820s and 1830s and was influenced by American Romanticism and a religious movement known as Unitarianism. During the nineteenth century, New Englanders began moving away from the Puritanism of their colonial past and toward Unitarianism, which perceived God as a singular being and had an optimistic view of human nature. Ralph Waldo Emerson, who is now regarded as the father of Transcendentalism, was an ordained Unitarian minister, but eventually resigned because he came to feel that Unitarianism was too restrictive and did not sufficiently recognize what he characterized as "the universal soul," or the divine, within each person. He felt that a church or religious authority only served to impede one's direct personal connection to God, causing "the withdrawal of the soul."

5 In 1836, Emerson began a discussion group, along with three other disaffected Unitarian clergy members, that became known as the **Transcendental Club**. It was through this forum that Emerson and other Transcendentalists formulated and explored the ideas that they would later publish in books of essays, as well as the literary magazine *The Dial* (1840–1844). Transcendentalism held that there was a part of the self that transcended the physical senses and logic, was highly in tune with nature, and brought individuals a kind of direct, divine knowledge. Transcendentalism was marked by optimism, idealism, and intuition. Transcendentalists criticized materialism, which they viewed as a corrupting influence, and championed social reform. Other well-known Transcendentalists include Henry David Thoreau, who wrote *Walden; or, Life in the Woods*, and Margaret Fuller, who was a writer and early feminist.

NOTES

6 Transcendentalism, despite being a relatively short-lived movement, had a definitive impact on American culture. Transcendentalist literature and philosophy influenced Walt Whitman, Emily Dickinson, and Frederick Douglass. Transcendentalist ideas about social improvement contributed to the Age of Reform (1830–1850) and Thoreau's essay "Civil Disobedience" informed the thinking of leaders such as Martin Luther King Jr.

Romanticism and Transcendentalism in Art

7 In Romanticism and Transcendentalism, creativity was highly esteemed. Painters used **symbolism** and **allegory** in their attempts to capture the essence of the sublime, or the essence of greatness. American Romantic painters from the Hudson River School looked to the vast and breathtaking American wilderness for inspiration and elevated landscape painting to the level of high art.

8 Major Concepts

- **Optimism and Individualism** — Romantics and Transcendentalists advocated individualism, but that didn't mean that they were selfish. They were also fiercely optimistic, and, for them, individualism and optimism went hand-in-hand. They believed that every individual possessed a natural inclination toward truth and spiritual enlightenment and that every person had the ability to rise above the material and emotional clutter of life in order to reflect on their lives and take individual action toward a greater good.
- **Kinship with Nature** — Both American Romantics and Transcendentalists believed that a close connection between humanity and nature brought humans closer to their true selves. This belief was complimented by a concern that the spread of industry not only threatened the natural world, but also isolated people from it. Furthermore, Transcendentalists felt that when individuals were detached from nature they also risked disconnection from the divine.
- **The Power of Darkness** — The Romantic fascination with emotion and the supernatural led to darker themes, as well. The Gothic and Horror genres took an interest in fear, madness, death, evil, and the destructive aspects of nature. The Dark Romantics, such as Nathaniel Hawthorne, Edgar Allan Poe, and Herman Melville, also contemplated sin, the nature of human fallibility, and the intrinsic challenges of social reform.

NOTES

Frankenstein and his Creature

Style and Form

9 Essays

- Transcendentalism was more than a genre; it was a philosophy. Transcendentalists were critical thinkers who explored many of their ideas through essays, short pieces of writing that attempted to grapple with an idea, explain something, or argue a point.

- The essay "Nature" (1836) by Ralph Waldo Emerson was the first essay to expound on the ideals of Transcendentalism. In the essay, Emerson set out to address one of Transcendentalism's defining concepts: the individual's relationship to nature. Emerson's abundant natural imagery and deeply felt personal connection to nature infused the otherwise serious philosophical tone of the piece with beauty, color, and life.

- The primary subject of Henry David Thoreau's work was the natural world. Many of his essays and books were structured as a literal or metaphorical journey. Essays such as "A Winter Walk" or "A Walk to Wachusett" were structured as small travelogues based on walks Thoreau had taken. Others, such as "Autumn Tints," "Wild Apples," or "A Succession of Forest Trees," journeyed through the cycles of nature. In his writings, Thoreau made scientific observations about nature, but also used natural imagery metaphorically and poetically. His sentences tended to be long and digressive. Thoreau was also a passionate abolitionist. His persuasive essays on the subject, including "Civil Disobedience," are still influential today.

10 Poet-Prophet

- The idea of the poet-prophet during the American Romantic period was defined by Emerson in his 1844 essay, "The Poet." Emerson saw poets as spiritual visionaries and "liberating gods." The poet, he said, interpreted nature—the thing that brought an individual closest to the divine—for society. According to Emerson, the highest form of language was the language of nature, which incorporated symbols related to the natural world as well as *synecdoche*, or the use of a part to represent the whole or vice versa. Emerson felt that the American literary landscape lacked such a visionary and ended "The Poet" with an impassioned call for a uniquely American poet-prophet.

- In 1855, the first edition of *Leaves of Grass* was published and Walt Whitman became America's own poetic visionary. Whitman's personal beliefs most closely resembled Transcendentalism and he was well versed in the work of Emerson, but he also had a broad understanding of American and European religious traditions, language, and symbolism, which he used stylistically in his poetry. He employed traditional symbols such as the stars, moon, and earth, but also created his own symbology, which included lilacs, the calamus plant, and, of course, grass. Whitman's tone was exuberant and his diction, or word choice, is notable for its eccentricities; he used colloquial words, foreign words, technical words, and sometimes even made up his own words. Whitman thought poetry should be read aloud and he was particularly attentive to sound imagery. Whitman's poetry did not rhyme and did not fit into any formal category, it followed the free and energetic path of Whitman's own mind and emotions. Today we call this informal structure **free verse**.

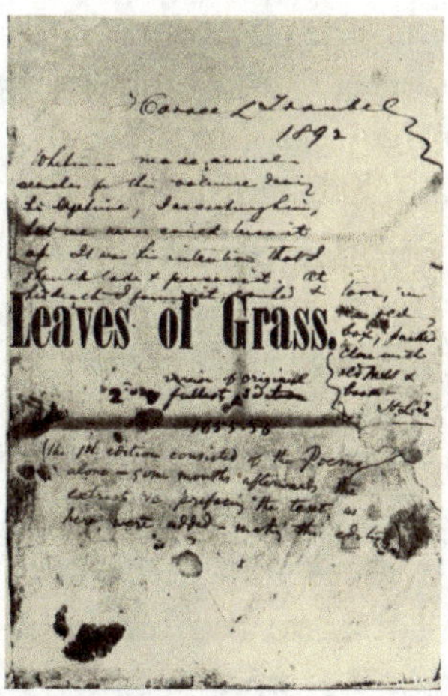

Leaves of Grass by Walt Whitman

NOTES

11 **Free Verse**

- It is not surprising that free-verse poetry rose to popularity during the American Romantic period when artists sought to reject the restrictive customs of the past in order to embrace liberation, individualism, imagination, intuition, and spiritual transcendence. Free verse is a non-metrical, non-rhyming form of poetry that tends to follow the natural cadence of speech. While a pattern of sound or rhythm may form within a free-verse poem, giving the poem its own unique structure, the poet does not plan or write the poem with any specific, preset poetic form in mind.

- Walt Whitman popularized the use of free verse, which has become one of the most frequently used forms of poetry in American literature and has been practiced, either on the whole or in part, by many American poets, including Emily Dickinson, Langston Hughes, Marianne Moore, Wallace Stevens, William Carlos Williams, Gwendolyn Brooks, Allen Ginsberg, Luis Omar Salinas, Pat Mora, and Nikki Giovanni, among many others.

12 **Nature**

- Romanticism and Transcendentalism are centered on a reverence for nature. The literature of these movements used abundant natural imagery and symbolism as well as sensory imagery, which endeavored to bring the sounds, sights, and feelings of nature to the reader. Nature not only served as a necessary counterbalance to the sweep of industrialization, urbanization, and materialism, but the Transcendentalists believed that nature, above all else, connected man to the divine within himself.

- The Dark Romantics used the weather, the tempestuous sea, nocturnal or menacing animals, and the frightening mysteries of the natural world in their imagery and settings. Poe's poem "The Raven" used the bird as a prophet of darkness, which drove the narrator to madness. Herman Melville's *Moby-Dick* takes place on a whaling ship in the lonely isolation of a vast seascape and the white whale is a complex symbol used to represent the nature of good and evil.

13 So where's the romance? American Romanticism and Transcendentalism are not about romance, per se, but they do have something to do with love—the love of truth, the love of beauty, and the love of nature. Like romantic love, Romanticism is characterized by optimism, idealism, and intuition. Romanticism and Transcendentalism, however, direct all of this love and optimism not toward another person, but toward the natural world and the divine within ourselves. The ideals of "big R" Romanticism, as well as Transcendentalism, are woven into the fabric of the American psyche. We can see their effects in movies about people who retreat to nature to become closer to themselves or reassess their life's purpose. We see these themes played out in stories about rugged individualists.

NOTES

14 Which of your favorite books or stories incorporate ideas from the American Romantic period? Is there someone in your life who you think embodies some facet of American Romanticism or Transcendentalism? How do you disconnect from technology, the material world, and the distractions of everyday life?

Literary Focus

Read "Literary Focus: Transcendentalism and Romanticism." After you read, complete the Think Questions below.

THINK QUESTIONS

1. How are Romanticism and Transcendentalism connected? What do the two periods or philosophies have in common? Be sure to use evidence from the text to support your response.

2. Which major concepts of Romanticism and Transcendentalism continue to be influential or important in the culture and art of today? Give specific examples.

3. "Transcendentalism was more than a genre; it was a philosophy." Explain how the ideals of the Transcendentalist movement connected to the writing forms that gained popularity during that period. Use evidence from this informational piece to back up your explanation.

4. What is the meaning of **Romanticism** as it used in this text? Write your own definition of the word, along with a brief explanation of how you came to that conclusion.

5. The word **allegory** comes from the Greek word *allēgorein*, which means to speak figuratively. With this information in mind and using context from the text, write your best definition of *allegory*, along with any words or phrases that were helpful in determining its meaning. Finally, check a dictionary to confirm your understanding.

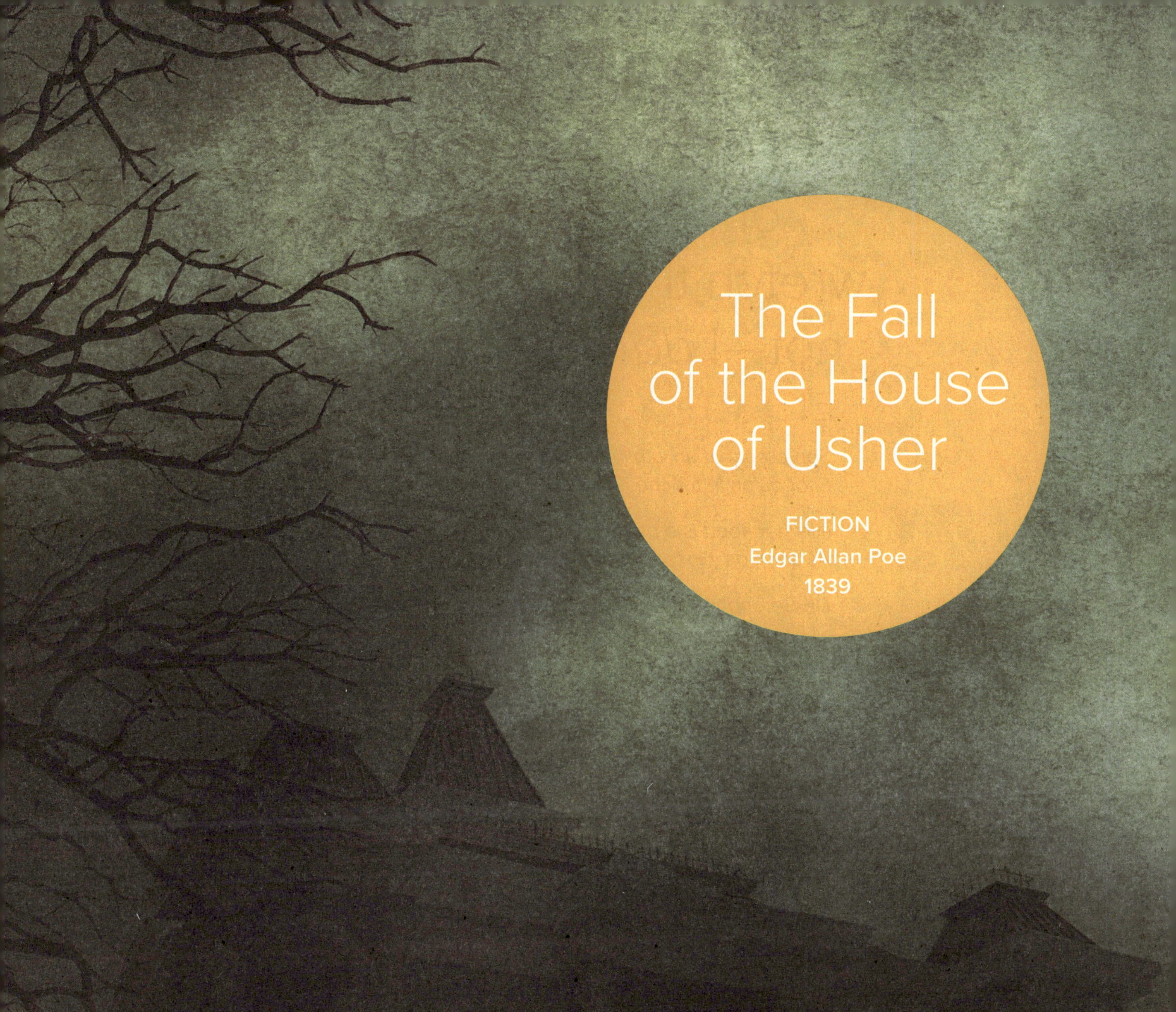

The Fall of the House of Usher

FICTION
Edgar Allan Poe
1839

Introduction

Edgar Allan Poe (1809–1849), aside from inventing the detective story, was also one of the early innovators of Gothic horror. "The Fall of the House of Usher" is one of Poe's most famous short stories, containing many familiar elements readers will encounter throughout his work: the innocent narrator called on for help; the family curse; the creepy, disintegrating old house; and a mysterious body of water (the *tarn*) that contains a possible source of evil. These now-familiar *tropes*, as they are called, continue to appear in horror novels, stories, and films to the present day. It was all here, first, brought to life by Poe's no-holds-barred language and his commitment to the lurid scare.

"... oh, pity me, miserable wretch that I am!—I dared not—I *dared* not speak!"

NOTES

Son cœur est un luth suspendu;
Sitôt qu'on le touche il résonne.

(His/her heart is a poised lute;
As soon as it is touched, it resounds)

De Béranger.

Edgar Allan Poe

1 During the whole of a dull, dark, and soundless day in the autumn of the year, when the clouds hung oppressively low in the heavens, I had been passing alone, on horseback, through a singularly dreary tract of country, and at length found myself, as the shades of the evening drew on, within view of the melancholy House of Usher. I know not how it was—but, with the first glimpse of the building, a sense of **insufferable** gloom pervaded my spirit. I say insufferable; for the feeling was unrelieved by any of that half-pleasurable, because poetic, sentiment, with which the mind usually receives even the sternest natural images of the desolate or terrible. I looked upon the scene before me—upon the mere house, and the simple landscape features of the domain—upon the bleak walls—upon the vacant eye-like windows—upon a few rank sedges—and upon a few white trunks of decayed trees—with an utter depression of soul which I can compare to no earthly sensation more properly than to the after-dream of the reveller upon opium—the bitter lapse into every-day life—the hideous dropping off of the veil. There was an iciness, a sinking, a sickening of the heart—an unredeemed dreariness of thought which no goading of the imagination could torture into aught of the sublime. What was it—I paused to think—what was it that so unnerved me in the contemplation of the House of Usher? It was a mystery all insoluble; nor could I grapple with the shadowy fancies that crowded upon me as I pondered. I was forced to fall back upon the unsatisfactory conclusion, that while, beyond doubt, there *are* combinations of very simple natural objects which have the power of thus affecting us, still the analysis of this power lies among considerations beyond

NOTES

our depth. It was possible, I reflected, that a mere different arrangement of the particulars of the scene, of the details of the picture, would be sufficient to modify, or perhaps to annihilate its capacity for sorrowful impression; and, acting upon this idea, I reined my horse to the precipitous brink of a black and lurid tarn that lay in unruffled lustre by the dwelling, and gazed down—but with a shudder even more thrilling than before—upon the remodelled and inverted images of the gray sedge, and the ghastly tree-stems, and the vacant and eye-like windows.

2 Nevertheless, in this mansion of gloom I now proposed to myself a sojourn of some weeks. Its proprietor, Roderick Usher, had been one of my boon companions in boyhood; but many years had elapsed since our last meeting. A letter, however, had lately reached me in a distant part of the country—a letter from him—which, in its wildly importunate nature, had admitted of no other than a personal reply. The MS. gave evidence of nervous agitation. The writer spoke of acute bodily illness—of a mental disorder which oppressed him—and of an earnest desire to see me, as his best and indeed his only personal friend, with a view of attempting, by the cheerfulness of my society, some alleviation of his **malady**. It was the manner in which all this, and much more, was said—it was the apparent *heart* that went with his request—which allowed me no room for hesitation; and I accordingly obeyed forthwith what I still considered a very singular summons.

3 Although, as boys, we had been even intimate associates, yet I really knew little of my friend. His reserve had been always excessive and habitual. I was aware, however, that his very ancient family had been noted, time out of mind, for a peculiar sensibility of temperament, displaying itself, through long ages, in many works of exalted art, and manifested, of late, in repeated deeds of **munificent** yet unobtrusive charity, as well as in a passionate devotion to the intricacies, perhaps even more than to the orthodox and easily recognizable beauties, of musical science. I had learned, too, the very remarkable fact, that the stem of the Usher race, all time-honored as it was, had put forth, at no period, any enduring branch; in other words, that the entire family lay in the direct line of descent, and had always, with very trifling and very temporary variation, so lain. It was this deficiency, I considered, while running over in thought the perfect keeping of the character of the premises with the accredited character of the people, and while speculating upon the possible influence which the one, in the long lapse of centuries, might have exercised upon the other—it was this deficiency, perhaps, of collateral issue, and the consequent undeviating transmission, from sire to son, of the patrimony with the name, which had, at length, so identified the two as to merge the original title of the estate in the quaint and equivocal appellation of the "House of Usher"—an appellation which seemed to include, in the minds of the peasantry who used it, both the family and the family mansion.

NOTES

4 I have said that the sole effect of my somewhat childish experiment—that of looking down within the tarn—had been to deepen the first singular impression. There can be no doubt that the consciousness of the rapid increase of my superstition—for why should I not so term it?—served mainly to accelerate the increase itself. Such, I have long known, is the paradoxical law of all sentiments having terror as a basis. And it might have been for this reason only, that, when I again uplifted my eyes to the house itself, from its image in the pool, there grew in my mind a strange fancy—a fancy so ridiculous, indeed, that I but mention it to show the vivid force of the sensations which oppressed me. I had so worked upon my imagination as really to believe that about the whole mansion and domain there hung an atmosphere peculiar to themselves and their immediate vicinity—an atmosphere which had no affinity with the air of heaven, but which had reeked up from the decayed trees, and the gray wall, and the silent tarn—a pestilent and mystic vapor, dull, sluggish, faintly discernible, and leaden-hued.

5 Shaking off from my spirit what *must* have been a dream, I scanned more narrowly the real aspect of the building. Its principal feature seemed to be that of an excessive antiquity. The discoloration of ages had been great. Minute fungi overspread the whole exterior, hanging in a fine tangled web-work from the eaves. Yet all this was apart from any extraordinary dilapidation. No portion of the masonry had fallen; and there appeared to be a wild inconsistency between its still perfect adaptation of parts, and the crumbling condition of the individual stones. In this there was much that reminded me of the specious totality of old wood-work which has rotted for long years in some neglected vault, with no disturbance from the breath of the external air. Beyond this indication of extensive decay, however, the fabric gave little token of instability. Perhaps the eye of a scrutinizing observer might have discovered a barely perceptible fissure, which, extending from the roof of the building in front, made its way down the wall in a zigzag direction, until it became lost in the sullen waters of the tarn.

6 Noticing these things, I rode over a short causeway to the house. A servant in waiting took my horse, and I entered the Gothic archway of the hall. A valet, of **stealthy** step, thence conducted me, in silence, through many dark and intricate passages in my progress to the *studio* of his master. Much that I encountered on the way contributed, I know not how, to heighten the vague sentiments of which I have already spoken. While the objects around me—while the carvings of the ceilings, the sombre tapestries of the walls, the ebon blackness of the floors, and the phantasmagoric armorial trophies which rattled as I strode, were but matters to which, or to such as which, I had been accustomed from my infancy—while I hesitated not to acknowledge how familiar was all this—I still wondered to find how unfamiliar were the fancies which ordinary images were stirring up. On one of the staircases, I met the physician of the family. His

NOTES

countenance, I thought, wore a mingled expression of low cunning and perplexity. He accosted me with **trepidation** and passed on. The valet now threw open a door and ushered me into the presence of his master.

7 The room in which I found myself was very large and lofty. The windows were long, narrow, and pointed, and at so vast a distance from the black oaken floor as to be altogether inaccessible from within. Feeble gleams of encrimsoned light made their way through the trellised panes, and served to render sufficiently distinct the more prominent objects around; the eye, however, struggled in vain to reach the remoter angles of the chamber, or the recesses of the vaulted and fretted ceiling. Dark draperies hung upon the walls. The general furniture was profuse, comfortless, antique, and tattered. Many books and musical instruments lay scattered about, but failed to give any vitality to the scene. I felt that I breathed an atmosphere of sorrow. An air of stern, deep, and irredeemable gloom hung over and pervaded all.

8 Upon my entrance, Usher rose from a sofa on which he had been lying at full length, and greeted me with a vivacious warmth which had much in it, I at first thought, of an overdone cordiality—of the constrained effort of the *ennuyé* man of the world. A glance, however, at his countenance convinced me of his perfect sincerity. We sat down; and for some moments, while he spoke not, I gazed upon him with a feeling half of pity, half of awe. Surely, man had never before so terribly altered, in so brief a period, as had Roderick Usher! It was with difficulty that I could bring myself to admit the identity of the wan being before me with the companion of my early boyhood. Yet the character of his face had been at all times remarkable. A cadaverousness of complexion; an eye large, liquid, and luminous beyond comparison; lips somewhat thin and very pallid, but of a surpassingly beautiful curve; a nose of a delicate Hebrew model, but with a breadth of nostril unusual in similar formations; a finely moulded chin, speaking, in its want of prominence, of a want of moral energy; hair of a more than web-like softness and tenuity;—these features, with an inordinate expansion above the regions of the temple, made up altogether a countenance not easily to be forgotten. And now in the mere exaggeration of the prevailing character of these features, and of the expression they were wont to convey, lay so much of change that I doubted to whom I spoke. The now ghastly pallor of the skin, and the now miraculous lustre of the eye, above all things startled and even awed me. The silken hair, too, had been suffered to grow all unheeded, and as, in its wild gossamer texture, it floated rather than fell about the face, I could not, even with effort, connect its Arabesque expression with any idea of simple humanity.

9 In the manner of my friend I was at once struck with an incoherence—an inconsistency; and I soon found this to arise from a series of feeble and futile struggles to overcome an habitual trepidancy—an excessive nervous

NOTES

agitation. For something of this nature I had indeed been prepared, no less by his letter, than by reminiscences of certain boyish traits, and by conclusions deduced from his peculiar physical conformation and temperament. His action was alternately vivacious and sullen. His voice varied rapidly from a tremulous indecision (when the animal spirits seemed utterly in abeyance) to that species of energetic concision—that abrupt, weighty, unhurried, and hollow-sounding enunciation—that leaden, self-balanced and perfectly modulated guttural utterance, which may be observed in the lost drunkard, or the irreclaimable eater of opium, during the periods of his most intense excitement.

10 It was thus that he spoke of the object of my visit, of his earnest desire to see me, and of the solace he expected me to afford him. He entered, at some length, into what he conceived to be the nature of his malady. It was, he said, a constitutional and a family evil, and one for which he despaired to find a remedy—a mere nervous affection, he immediately added, which would undoubtedly soon pass off. It displayed itself in a host of unnatural sensations. Some of these, as he detailed them, interested and bewildered me; although, perhaps, the terms and the general manner of the narration had their weight. He suffered much from a morbid acuteness of the senses; the most insipid food was alone endurable; he could wear only garments of certain texture; the odors of all flowers were oppressive; his eyes were tortured by even a faint light; and there were but peculiar sounds, and these from stringed instruments, which did not inspire him with horror.

11 To an anomalous species of terror I found him a bounden slave. "I shall perish," said he, "I *must* perish in this deplorable folly. Thus, thus, and not otherwise, shall I be lost. I dread the events of the future, not in themselves, but in their results. I shudder at the thought of any, even the most trivial, incident, which may operate upon this intolerable agitation of soul. I have, indeed, no abhorrence of danger, except in its absolute effect—in terror. In this unnerved, in this pitiable, condition I feel that the period will sooner or later arrive when I must abandon life and reason together, in some struggle with the grim phantasm, FEAR."

12 I learned, moreover, at intervals, and through broken and equivocal hints, another singular feature of his mental condition. He was enchained by certain superstitious impressions in regard to the dwelling which he tenanted, and whence, for many years, he had never ventured forth—in regard to an influence whose supposititious force was conveyed in terms too shadowy here to be re-stated—an influence which some peculiarities in the mere form and substance of his family mansion had, by dint of long sufferance, he said, obtained over his spirit—an effect which the *physique* of the gray walls and

NOTES

turrets, and of the dim tarn into which they all looked down, had, at length, brought about upon the *morale* of his existence.

13 He admitted, however, although with hesitation, that much of the peculiar gloom which thus afflicted him could be traced to a more natural and far more palpable origin—to the severe and long-continued illness—indeed to the evidently approaching dissolution—of a tenderly beloved sister, his sole companion for long years, his last and only relative on earth. "Her decease," he said, with a bitterness which I can never forget, "would leave him (him the hopeless and the frail) the last of the ancient race of the Ushers." While he spoke, the lady Madeline (for so was she called) passed slowly through a remote portion of the apartment, and, without having noticed my presence, disappeared. I regarded her with an utter astonishment not unmingled with dread; and yet I found it impossible to account for such feelings. A sensation of stupor oppressed me as my eyes followed her retreating steps. When a door, at length, closed upon her, my glance sought instinctively and eagerly the countenance of the brother; but he had buried his face in his hands, and I could only perceive that a far more than ordinary wanness had overspread the emaciated fingers through which trickled many passionate tears.

14 The disease of the lady Madeline had long baffled the skill of her physicians. A settled apathy, a gradual wasting away of the person, and frequent although transient affections of a partially cataleptical character were the unusual diagnosis. Hitherto she had steadily borne up against the pressure of her malady, and had not betaken herself finally to bed; but on the closing in of the evening of my arrival at the house, she succumbed (as her brother told me at night with inexpressible agitation) to the prostrating power of the destroyer; and I learned that the glimpse I had obtained of her person would thus probably be the last I should obtain—that the lady, at least while living, would be seen by me no more.

15 For several days ensuing, her name was unmentioned by either Usher or myself; and during this period I was busied in earnest endeavors to alleviate the melancholy of my friend. We painted and read together, or I listened, as if in a dream, to the wild improvisations of his speaking guitar. And thus, as a closer and still closer intimacy admitted me more unreservedly into the recesses of his spirit, the more bitterly did I perceive the futility of all attempt at cheering a mind from which darkness, as if an inherent positive quality, poured forth upon all objects of the moral and physical universe in one unceasing radiation of gloom.

16 I shall ever bear about me a memory of the many solemn hours I thus spent alone with the master of the House of Usher. Yet I should fail in any attempt to convey an idea of the exact character of the studies, or of the occupations,

NOTES

in which he involved me, or led me the way. An excited and highly distempered ideality threw a sulphureous lustre over all. His long improvised dirges will ring forever in my ears. Among other things, I hold painfully in mind a certain singular perversion and amplification of the wild air of the last waltz of Von Weber[1]. From the paintings over which his elaborate fancy brooded, and which grew, touch by touch, into vagueness at which I shuddered the more thrillingly, because I shuddered knowing not why—from these paintings (vivid as their images now are before me) I would in vain endeavor to deduce more than a small portion which should lie within the compass of merely written words. By the utter simplicity, by the nakedness of his designs, he arrested and overawed attention. If ever mortal painted an idea, that mortal was Roderick Usher. For me at least, in the circumstances then surrounding me, there arose out of the pure abstractions which the hypochondriac contrived to throw upon his canvas, an intensity of intolerable awe, no shadow of which felt I ever yet in the contemplation of the certainly glowing yet too concrete reveries of Fuseli[2].

17 One of the phantasmagoric conceptions of my friend, partaking not so rigidly of the spirit of abstraction, may be shadowed forth, although feebly, in words. A small picture presented the interior of an immensely long and rectangular vault or tunnel, with low walls, smooth, white, and without interruption or device. Certain accessory points of the design served well to convey the idea that this excavation lay at an exceeding depth below the surface of the earth. No outlet was observed in any portion of its vast extent, and no torch or other artificial source of light was discernible; yet a flood of intense rays rolled throughout, and bathed the whole in a ghastly and inappropriate splendor.

18 I have just spoken of that morbid condition of the auditory nerve which rendered all music intolerable to the sufferer, with the exception of certain effects of stringed instruments. It was, perhaps, the narrow limits to which he thus confined himself upon the guitar which gave birth, in great measure, to the fantastic character of the performances. But the fervid *facility* of his *impromptus* could not be so accounted for. They must have been, and were, in the notes, as well as in the words of his wild fantasias (for he not unfrequently accompanied himself with rhymed verbal improvisations), the result of that intense mental collectedness and concentration to which I have previously alluded as observable only in particular moments of the highest artificial excitement. The words of one of these rhapsodies I have easily remembered. I was, perhaps, the more forcibly impressed with it as he gave it, because, in the under or mystic current of its meaning, I fancied that I perceived, and for the first time, a full consciousness on the part of Usher of the tottering of his

1. **the last waltz of Von Weber** a famous piece of classical music
2. **Fuseli** a Dutch painter working in the early 19th century, many of whose paintings dealt with supernatural or mythological subject matter

NOTES

lofty reason upon her throne. The verses, which were entitled "The Haunted Palace," ran very nearly, if not accurately, thus:

I.
19 In the greenest of our valleys,
By good angels tenanted,
Once a fair and stately palace—
Radiant palace—reared its head.
In the monarch Thought's dominion—
It stood there!
Never seraph spread a pinion
Over fabric half so fair.
II.
20 Banners yellow, glorious, golden,
On its roof did float and flow;
(This—all this—was in the olden
Time long ago);
And every gentle air that dallied,
In that sweet day,
Along the ramparts plumed and pallid,
A winged odor went away.

III.
21 Wanderers in that happy valley
Through two luminous windows saw
Spirits moving musically
To a lute's well-tunèd law;
Round about a throne, where sitting
(Porphyrogene![3])
In state his glory well befitting,
The ruler of the realm was seen.

IV.
22 And all with pearl and ruby glowing
Was the fair palace door,
Through which came flowing, flowing, flowing
And sparkling evermore,
A troop of Echoes[4] whose sweet duty
Was but to sing,
In voices of surpassing beauty,
The wit and wisdom of their king.

---

3. **Porphyrogene** literally "born into purple," purple in this context representing royalty or nobility
4. **Echo** in Greek mythology, a cave nymph who was cursed by Hera, Zeus's wife, to repeat other people's previous words

NOTES

V.

23 But evil things, in robes of sorrow,
Assailed the monarch's high estate;
(Ah, let us mourn, for never morrow
Shall dawn upon him, desolate!)
And, round about his home, the glory
That blushed and bloomed
Is but a dim-remembered story
Of the old time entombed.

VI.

24 And travellers now within that valley,
Through the red-litten windows see
Vast forms that move fantastically
To a discordant melody;
While, like a rapid ghastly river,
Through the pale door,
A hideous throng rush out forever,
And laugh—but smile no more.

25 I well remember that suggestions arising from this ballad, led us into a train of thought wherein there became manifest an opinion of Usher's which I mention not so much on account of its novelty (for other men have thought thus), as on account of the pertinacity with which he maintained it. This opinion, in its general form, was that of the sentience of all vegetable things. But, in his disordered fancy, the idea had assumed a more daring character, and trespassed, under certain conditions, upon the kingdom of inorganization. I lack words to express the full extent, or the earnest *abandon* of his persuasion. The belief, however, was connected (as I have previously hinted) with the gray stones of the home of his forefathers. The conditions of the sentience had been here, he imagined, fulfilled in the method of collocation of these stones—in the order of their arrangement, as well as in that of the many *fungi* which overspread them, and of the decayed trees which stood around—above all, in the long undisturbed endurance of this arrangement, and in its reduplication in the still waters of the tarn. Its evidence—the evidence of the sentience—was to be seen, he said, (and I here started as he spoke), in the gradual yet certain condensation of an atmosphere of their own about the waters and the walls. The result was discoverable, he added, in that silent yet importunate and terrible influence which for centuries had moulded the destinies of his family, and which made *him* what I now saw him—what he was. Such opinions need no comment, and I will make none.

26 Our books—the books which, for years, had formed no small portion of the mental existence of the invalid—were, as might be supposed, in strict keeping with this character of phantasm. We pored together over such works as the

NOTES

Ververt et Chartreuse of Gresset; the Belphegor of Machiavelli; the Heaven and Hell of Swedenborg; the Subterranean Voyage of Nicholas Klimm by Holberg; the Chiromancy of Robert Flud, of Jean D'Indaginé, and of De la Chambre; the Journey into the Blue Distance of Tieck; and the City of the Sun of Campanella. One favorite volume was a small octavo edition of the Directorium Inquisitorium, by the Dominican Eymeric de Gironne; and there were passages in Pomponius Mela, about the old African Satyrs and Œgipans, over which Usher would sit dreaming for hours. His chief delight, however, was found in the perusal of an exceedingly rare and curious book in quarto Gothic—the manual of a forgotten church—the Vigiliæ Mortuorum Secundum Chorum Ecclesiæ Maguntinæ[5].

27 I could not help thinking of the wild ritual of this work, and of its probable influence upon the hypochondriac, when, one evening, having informed me abruptly that the lady Madeline was no more, he stated his intention of preserving her corpse for a fortnight (previously to its final interment), in one of the numerous vaults within the main walls of the building. The worldly reason, however, assigned for this singular proceeding, was one which I did not feel at liberty to dispute. The brother had been led to his resolution (so he told me) by consideration of the unusual character of the malady of the deceased, of certain obtrusive and eager inquiries on the part of her medical men, and of the remote and exposed situation of the burial-ground of the family. I will not deny that when I called to mind the sinister countenance of the person whom I met upon the staircase, on the day of my arrival at the house, I had no desire to oppose what I regarded as at best but a harmless, and by no means an unnatural, precaution.

28 At the request of Usher, I personally aided him in the arrangements for the temporary entombment. The body having been encoffined, we two alone bore it to its rest. The vault in which we placed it (and which had been so long unopened that our torches, half smothered in its oppressive atmosphere, gave us little opportunity for investigation) was small, damp, and entirely without means of admission for light; lying, at great depth, immediately beneath that portion of the building in which was my own sleeping apartment. It had been used, apparently, in remote feudal times, for the worst purposes of a donjon-keep, and, in later days, as a place of deposit for powder, or some other highly combustible substance, as a portion of its floor, and the whole interior of a long archway through which we reached it, were carefully sheathed with copper. The door, of massive iron, had been, also, similarly protected. Its immense weight caused an unusually sharp, grating sound, as it moved upon its hinges.

5. **Vigiliæ Mortuorum Secundum Chorum Ecclesiæ Maguntinæ** the title of a book printed in 1500, translated from Latin: "Vigils for the Dead According to the Use of the Church of Mainz"

NOTES

29 Having deposited our mournful burden upon tressels within this region of horror, we partially turned aside the yet unscrewed lid of the coffin, and looked upon the face of the tenant. A striking similitude between the brother and sister now first arrested my attention; and Usher, divining, perhaps, my thoughts, murmured out some few words from which I learned that the deceased and himself had been twins, and that sympathies of a scarcely intelligible nature had always existed between them. Our glances, however, rested not long upon the dead—for we could not regard her unawed. The disease which had thus entombed the lady in the maturity of youth, had left, as usual in all maladies of a strictly cataleptical character, the mockery of a faint blush upon the bosom and the face, and that suspiciously lingering smile upon the lip which is so terrible in death. We replaced and screwed down the lid, and, having secured the door of iron, made our way, with toil, into the scarcely less gloomy apartments of the upper portion of the house.

30 And now, some days of bitter grief having elapsed, an observable change came over the features of the mental disorder of my friend. His ordinary manner had vanished. His ordinary occupations were neglected or forgotten. He roamed from chamber to chamber with hurried, unequal, and objectless step. The pallor of his countenance had assumed, if possible, a more ghastly hue—but the luminousness of his eye had utterly gone out. The once occasional huskiness of his tone was heard no more; and a tremulous quaver, as if of extreme terror, habitually characterized his utterance. There were times, indeed, when I thought his unceasingly agitated mind was laboring with some oppressive secret, to divulge which he struggled for the necessary courage. At times, again, I was obliged to resolve all into the mere inexplicable vagaries of madness, for I beheld him gazing upon vacancy for long hours, in an attitude of the profoundest attention, as if listening to some imaginary sound. It was no wonder that his condition terrified—that it infected me. I felt creeping upon me, by slow yet certain degrees, the wild influences of his own fantastic yet impressive superstitions.

31 It was, especially, upon retiring to bed late in the night of the seventh or eighth day after the placing of the lady Madeline within the donjon, that I experienced the full power of such feelings. Sleep came not near my couch—while the hours waned and waned away. I struggled to reason off the nervousness which had dominion over me. I endeavored to believe that much, if not all of what I felt, was due to the bewildering influence of the gloomy furniture of the room—of the dark and tattered draperies, which, tortured into motion by the breath of a rising tempest, swayed fitfully to and fro upon the walls, and rustled uneasily about the decorations of the bed. But my efforts were fruitless. An irrepressible tremor gradually pervaded my frame; and, at length, there sat upon my very heart an incubus of utterly causeless alarm. Shaking this off with a gasp and a struggle, I uplifted myself upon the pillows, and, peering earnestly within the intense darkness of the

NOTES

chamber, hearkened—I know not why, except that an instinctive spirit prompted me—to certain low and indefinite sounds which came, through the pauses of the storm, at long intervals, I knew not whence. Overpowered by an intense sentiment of horror, unaccountable yet unendurable, I threw on my clothes with haste (for I felt that I should sleep no more during the night), and endeavored to arouse myself from the pitiable condition into which I had fallen, by pacing rapidly to and fro through the apartment.

32 I had taken but few turns in this manner, when a light step on an adjoining staircase arrested my attention. I presently recognized it as that of Usher. In an instant afterward he rapped, with a gentle touch, at my door, and entered, bearing a lamp. His countenance was, as usual, cadaverously wan—but, moreover, there was a species of mad hilarity in his eyes—an evidently restrained *hysteria* in his whole demeanor. His air appalled me—but anything was preferable to the solitude which I had so long endured, and I even welcomed his presence as a relief.

33 "And you have not seen it?" he said abruptly, after having stared about him for some moments in silence—"you have not then seen it?—but, stay! you shall." Thus speaking, and having carefully shaded his lamp, he hurried to one of the casements[6], and threw it freely open to the storm.

34 The impetuous fury of the entering gust nearly lifted us from our feet. It was, indeed, a tempestuous yet sternly beautiful night, and one wildly singular in its terror and its beauty. A whirlwind had apparently collected its force in our vicinity; for there were frequent and violent alterations in the direction of the wind; and the exceeding density of the clouds (which hung so low as to press upon the turrets of the house) did not prevent our perceiving the life-like velocity with which they flew careering from all points against each other, without passing away into the distance. I say that even their exceeding density did not prevent our perceiving this—yet we had no glimpse of the moon or stars, nor was there any flashing forth of the lightning. But the under surfaces of the huge masses of agitated vapor, as well as all terrestrial objects immediately around us, were glowing in the unnatural light of a faintly luminous and distinctly visible gaseous exhalation which hung about and enshrouded the mansion.

35 "You must not—you shall not behold this!" said I, shuddering, to Usher, as I led him, with a gentle violence, from the window to a seat. "These appearances, which bewilder you, are merely electrical phenomena not uncommon—or it may be that they have their ghastly origin in the rank miasma of the tarn. Let us close this casement;—the air is chilling and dangerous to your frame. Here

6. **casements** hinged windows

NOTES

is one of your favorite romances. I will read, and you shall listen:—and so we will pass away this terrible night together."

36 The antique volume which I had taken up was the "Mad Trist" of Sir Launcelot Canning[7]; but I had called it a favorite of Usher's more in sad jest than in earnest; for, in truth, there is little in its uncouth and unimaginative prolixity which could have had interest for the lofty and spiritual ideality of my friend. It was, however, the only book immediately at hand; and I indulged a vague hope that the excitement which now agitated the hypochondriac, might find relief (for the history of mental disorder is full of similar anomalies) even in the extremeness of the folly which I should read. Could I have judged, indeed, by the wild overstrained air of vivacity with which he hearkened, or apparently hearkened, to the words of the tale, I might well have congratulated myself upon the success of my design.

37 I had arrived at that well-known portion of the story where Ethelred, the hero of the Trist, having sought in vain for peaceable admission into the dwelling of the hermit, proceeds to make good an entrance by force. Here, it will be remembered, the words of the narrative run thus:

38 "And Ethelred, who was by nature of a doughty heart, and who was now mighty withal, on account of the powerfulness of the wine which he had drunken, waited no longer to hold parley with the hermit, who, in sooth, was of an obstinate and maliceful turn, but, feeling the rain upon his shoulders, and fearing the rising of the tempest, uplifted his mace outright, and, with blows, made quickly room in the plankings of the door for his gauntleted hand; and now pulling therewith sturdily, he so cracked, and ripped, and tore all asunder, that the noise of the dry and hollow-sounding wood alarumed and reverberated throughout the forest."

39 At the termination of this sentence I started and, for a moment, paused; for it appeared to me (although I at once concluded that my excited fancy had deceived me)—it appeared to me that, from some very remote portion of the mansion, there came, indistinctly to my ears, what might have been, in its exact similarity of character, the echo (but a stifled and dull one certainly) of the very cracking and ripping sound which Sir Launcelot had so particularly described. It was, beyond doubt, the coincidence alone which had arrested my attention; for, amid the rattling of the sashes of the casements, and the ordinary commingled noises of the still increasing storm, the sound, in itself, had nothing, surely, which should have interested or disturbed me. I continued the story:

7. **"Mad Trist" of Sir Launcelot Canning** a work of fiction written by Poe, which he attributed to Sir Launcelot Canning, who is also fictitious

NOTES

40 "But the good champion Ethelred, now entering within the door, was sore enraged and amazed to perceive no signal of the maliceful hermit; but, in the stead thereof, a dragon of a scaly and prodigious demeanor, and of a fiery tongue, which sate in guard before a palace of gold, with a floor of silver; and upon the wall there hung a shield of shining brass with this legend enwritten—

41 Who entereth herein, a conqueror hath bin;
Who slayeth the dragon, the shield he shall win.

42 And Ethelred uplifted his mace, and struck upon the head of the dragon, which fell before him, and gave up his pesty breath, with a shriek so horrid and harsh, and withal so piercing, that Ethelred had fain to close his ears with his hands against the dreadful noise of it, the like whereof was never before heard."

43 Here again I paused abruptly, and now with a feeling of wild amazement—for there could be no doubt whatever that, in this instance, I did actually hear (although from what direction it proceeded I found it impossible to say) a low and apparently distant, but harsh, protracted, and most unusual screaming or grating sound—the exact counterpart of what my fancy had already conjured up for the dragon's unnatural shriek as described by the romancer.

44 Oppressed, as I certainly was, upon the occurrence of this second and most extraordinary coincidence, by a thousand conflicting sensations, in which wonder and extreme terror were predominant, I still retained sufficient presence of mind to avoid exciting, by any observation, the sensitive nervousness of my companion. I was by no means certain that he had noticed the sounds in question; although, assuredly, a strange alteration had, during the last few minutes, taken place in his demeanor. From a position fronting my own, he had gradually brought round his chair, so as to sit with his face to the door of the chamber; and thus I could but partially perceive his features, although I saw that his lips trembled as if he were murmuring inaudibly. His head had dropped upon his breast—yet I knew that he was not asleep, from the wide and rigid opening of the eye as I caught a glance of it in profile. The motion of his body, too, was at variance with this idea—for he rocked from side to side with a gentle yet constant and uniform sway. Having rapidly taken notice of all this, I resumed the narrative of Sir Launcelot, which thus proceeded:

45 "And now, the champion, having escaped from the terrible fury of the dragon, bethinking himself of the brazen shield, and of the breaking up of the enchantment which was upon it, removed the carcass from out of the way before him, and approached valorously over the silver pavement of the castle to where the shield was upon the wall; which in sooth tarried not for his full coming, but fell down at his feet upon the silver floor, with a mighty great and terrible ringing sound."

NOTES

46 No sooner had these syllables passed my lips, than—as if a shield of brass had indeed, at the moment, fallen heavily upon a floor of silver—I became aware of a distinct, hollow, metallic, and clangorous, yet apparently muffled, reverberation. Completely unnerved, I leaped to my feet; but the measured rocking movement of Usher was undisturbed. I rushed to the chair in which he sat. His eyes were bent fixedly before him, and throughout his whole countenance there reigned a stony rigidity. But, as I placed my hand upon his shoulder, there came a strong shudder over his whole person; a sickly smile quivered about his lips; and I saw that he spoke in a low, hurried, and gibbering murmur, as if unconscious of my presence. Bending closely over him, I at length drank in the hideous import of his words.

47 "Not hear it?—yes, I hear it, and *have* heard it. Long—long—long—many minutes, many hours, many days, have I heard it—yet I dared not—oh, pity me, miserable wretch that I am!—I dared not—I *dared* not speak! *We have put her living in the tomb!* Said I not that my senses were acute? I *now* tell you that I heard her first feeble movements in the hollow coffin. I heard them—many, many days ago—yet I dared not—*I dared not speak!* And now—to-night—Ethelred—ha! ha!—the breaking of the hermit's door, and the death-cry of the dragon, and the clangor of the shield!—say, rather, the rending of her coffin, and the grating of the iron hinges of her prison, and her struggles within the coppered archway of the vault! Oh! whither shall I fly? Will she not be here anon? Is she not hurrying to upbraid me for my haste? Have I not heard her footstep on the stair? Do I not distinguish that heavy and horrible beating of her heart? Madman!"—here he sprang furiously to his feet, and shrieked out his syllables, as if in the effort he were giving up his soul—*"Madman! I tell you that she now stands without the door!"*

48 As if in the superhuman energy of his utterance there had been found the potency of a spell, the huge antique panels to which the speaker pointed threw slowly back, upon the instant, their ponderous and ebony jaws. It was the work of the rushing gust—but then without those doors there *did* stand the lofty and enshrouded figure of the lady Madeline of Usher. There was blood upon her white robes, and the evidence of some bitter struggle upon every portion of her emaciated frame. For a moment she remained trembling and reeling to and fro upon the threshold—then, with a low moaning cry, fell heavily inward upon the person of her brother, and in her violent and now final death-agonies, bore him to the floor a corpse, and a victim to the terrors he had anticipated.

49 From that chamber, and from that mansion, I fled aghast. The storm was still abroad in all its wrath as I found myself crossing the old causeway. Suddenly there shot along the path a wild light, and I turned to see whence a gleam so unusual could have issued; for the vast house and its shadows were alone behind me. The radiance was that of the full, setting, and blood-red moon

NOTES

which now shone vividly through that once barely-discernible fissure of which I have before spoken as extending from the roof of the building, in a zigzag direction, to the base. While I gazed, this fissure rapidly widened—there came a fierce breath of the whirlwind—the entire orb of the satellite burst at once upon my sight—my brain reeled as I saw the mighty walls rushing asunder—there was a long tumultuous shouting sound like the voice of a thousand waters—and the deep and dank tarn at my feet closed sullenly and silently over the fragments of the "*House of Usher.*"

WRITE

EXPLANATORY: In many horror stories and horror movies, a house serves as a symbol, and some may even consider the house a character. How is the house described in "The Fall of the House of Usher"? What does it symbolize? How does the house itself define the people who live in it? Why are houses that are haunted, dilapidated, or mysterious so common in the horror genre? Support your explanation using evidence from the text and original commentary.

Because I could not stop for Death

POETRY

Emily Dickinson

1890

Introduction

Beloved American poet Emily Dickinson (1830–1886) composed nearly 1,800 poems, but fewer than a dozen were published during her lifetime. The famously private Dickinson lived an untraditional lifestyle but held a deep understanding of the human condition. It shines through in "Because I could not stop for Death," her flawlessly written lyrical poem about death and what might follow.

"We slowly drove – He knew no haste"

Because I could not stop for Death –
He kindly stopped for me –
The Carriage held but just Ourselves –
And **Immortality**.

We slowly drove – He knew no haste
And I had put away
My labor and my leisure too,
For His **Civility** –

We passed the School, where Children strove
At Recess – in the Ring –
We passed the Fields of Gazing Grain –
We passed the Setting Sun –

Or rather – He passed us –
The Dews drew quivering and chill –
For only **Gossamer**, my Gown –
My Tippet[1] – only Tulle[2] –

We paused before a House that seemed
A Swelling of the Ground –
The Roof was scarcely visible –
The Cornice[3] – in the Ground –

Since then – 'tis Centuries – and yet
Feels shorter than the Day
I first **surmised** the Horses' Heads
Were toward **Eternity** –

NOTES

Skill: Figurative Language

Given the context of the poem, the author seems to be using the language about a school, fields, and the setting sun to symbolize a journey through a lifetime.

1. **Tippet** (old-fashioned) a shawl or cape
2. **Tulle** a soft, silk-like fabric
3. **Cornice** a molding or ornamental feature that outlines an architectural structure

First Read

Read "Because I could not stop for Death." After you read, complete the Think Questions below.

THINK QUESTIONS

1. Based on the first two stanzas of the poem, what inferences can you make about the speaker? Provide textual evidence that supports your response.

2. Look at the third stanza of the poem. How does the poet use repetition for effect in this stanza, in terms of both style and meaning? Cite direct quotations to help develop your explanation.

3. In what different ways is time referenced and represented in the poem? Provide details from the text to develop and support your ideas.

4. Keeping in mind that the Latin word *civis* means "citizen," determine the meaning of the word **civility** as it is used in line 8. Write your definition of *civility* here and explain which clues helped you determine the word's meaning.

5. Use context clues to determine the meaning of the word **eternity** as it is used in the final line. Write your definition of *eternity* here and explain which clues helped you figure it out.

Skill: Figurative Language

Use the Checklist to analyze Figurative Language in "Because I could not stop for Death." Refer to the sample student annotation about Figurative Language in the text.

••• CHECKLIST FOR FIGURATIVE LANGUAGE

In order to determine the meaning of a figure of speech in context, note the following:

- ✓ words that mean one thing literally and suggest something else
- ✓ similes, metaphors, or personification
- ✓ figures of speech, including
    - paradoxes, or a seemingly contradictory statement that when further investigated or explained proves to be true, such as
        - > a character described as "a wise fool"
        - > a character stating, "I must be cruel to be kind"
    - hyperbole, or exaggerated statements not meant to be taken literally, such as
        - > a child saying, "I'll be doing this homework until I'm 100!"
        - > a claim such as "I'm so hungry I could eat a horse!"

In order to interpret a figure of speech in context and analyze its role in the text, consider the following questions:

- ✓ Where is there figurative language in the text and what seems to be the purpose of the author's use of it?
- ✓ Why does the author use a figure of speech rather than literal language?
- ✓ What impact does exaggeration or hyperbole have on your understanding of the text?

- ✓ Where are there examples of paradoxes and how do they affect the meaning in the text?
- ✓ What phrases contain a reference that seems contradictory?
- ✓ Where are contradictory words and phrases used to enhance the reader's understanding of the character, object, or idea?
- ✓ How does the figurative language develop the message or theme of the literary work?

Skill: Figurative Language

Reread lines 13–18 of "Because I could not stop for Death." Then, using the Checklist on the previous pages, answer the multiple-choice questions below.

YOUR TURN

1. This question has two parts. First, answer Part A. Then, answer Part B.

Part A: Which of the following provides the best restatement of a metaphor within these two stanzas?

- O A. The dew makes everything wet.
- O B. The speaker's new home will be her grave.
- O C. Death has destroyed the entire world as well.
- O D. The speaker's gown is frayed.

Part B: Which of the following offers the best evidence of this metaphor within the passage?

- O A. "We paused before a House that seemed / A Swelling of the Ground —"
- O B. "Or rather – He passed us –"
- O C. "The Dews drew quivering and chill –"
- O D. "For only **Gossamer**, my Gown – / My Tippet – only Tulle –"

Close Read

Reread "Because I could not stop for Death." As you reread, complete the Skills Focus questions below. Then use your answers and annotations from the questions to help you complete the Write activity.

SKILLS FOCUS

1. Explain how the figurative and connotative meanings of the word *house* influence the tone of the poem.
2. Compare and contrast a line with a cheerful tone and a line with a more sorrowful tone as evidence to support your interpretation of the poem's overall theme.
3. Explain how the author's experiences might have informed her perspective in the poem. Cite evidence from the text to support your response.

WRITE

LITERARY ANALYSIS: Dickinson and Poe created pieces that recognize the complexity of mortality, using a variety of figurative language techniques to convey their messages. Select one example of figurative language from "Because I could not stop for Death" and another example from "The Fall of the House of Usher," and compare how these examples contribute to the overall meaning of each text. Use evidence from the text and original commentary to support your response.

Society and Solitude

INFORMATIONAL TEXT
Ralph Waldo Emerson
1857

Introduction

In the essay "Society and Solitude," Ralph Waldo Emerson (1803–1882) contemplates the nature of solitude and self-reliance in the real world, embracing independent thought and championing the individual. Emerson was an essayist and philosopher and the leader of the Transcendentalist movement in the mid-19th century. His work explores our effect on society and society's effect on us, stating that a sound mind will derive its principles from personal insight and interact with society accordingly.

"Solitude is impracticable, and society fatal."

NOTES

1 'Tis hard to mesmerize ourselves, to whip our own top; but through sympathy we are capable of energy and endurance. Concert fires people to a certain fury of performance they can rarely reach alone. Here is the use of society: it is so easy with the great to be great; so easy to come up to an existing standard;—as easy as it is to the lover to swim to his maiden through waves so **grim** before. The benefits of affection are immense; and the one event which never loses its romance, is the encounter with superior persons on terms allowing the happiest intercourse.

2 It by no means follows that we are not fit for society, because soirées[1] are **tedious**, and because the soirée finds us tedious. A backwoodsman, who had been sent to the university, told me that, when he heard the best-bred young men at the law school talk together, he reckoned himself a boor; but whenever he caught them apart, and had one to himself alone, then they were the boors, and he the better man. And if we recall the rare hours when we encountered the best persons, we then found ourselves, and then first society seemed to exist. That was society, though in the transom of a brig, or on the Florida Keys.

3 A cold, sluggish blood thinks it has not facts enough to the purpose, and must decline its turn in the conversation. But they who speak have no more,—have less. 'Tis not new facts that avail, but the heat to dissolve everybody's facts.

4 The capital defect of cold, arid natures is the want of animal spirits. They seem a power incredible, as if God should raise the dead. The **recluse** witnesses what others perform by their aid, with a kind of fear. It is as much out of his possibility as the prowess of Coeur-de-Lion[2], or an Irishman's day's-work on the railroad. 'Tis said, the present and the future are always rivals. Animal spirits constitute the power of the present, and their feats are like the structure of a pyramid. Their result is a lord, a general, or a boon companion.

1. **soirées** evening parties, most often held in a private house, for the purpose of conversation or music
2. **Coeur-de-Lion** a symbol of bravery and courage, popularized by French historians of the 12th century, who attributed this nickname to King Richard I of England

NOTES

Before these, what a base mendicant[3] is Memory with his leathern badge! But this genial heat is **latent** in all constitutions, and is disengaged only by the friction of society. As Bacon[4] said of manners, "To obtain them, it only needs not to despise them," so we say of animal spirits, that they are the spontaneous product of health and of a social habit. "For behavior, men learn it, as they take diseases, one of another."

5 But the people are to be taken in very small doses. If solitude is proud, so is society vulgar. In society, high advantages are set down to the individual as disqualifications. We sink as easily as we rise, through sympathy. So many men whom I know are degraded by their sympathies, their native aims being high enough, but their relation all too tender to the gross people about them. Men cannot afford to live together by their merits, and they adjust themselves by their demerits,—by their love of gossip, or by sheer **tolerance** and animal good-nature. They untune and dissipate the brave aspirant.

6 The remedy is, to reinforce each of these moods from the other. Conversation will not corrupt us, if we come to the assembly in our own garb and speech, and with the energy of health to select what is ours and reject what is not.

7 Society we must have; but let it be society, and not exchanging news, or eating from the same dish. Is it society to sit in one of your chairs? I cannot go into the houses of my nearest relatives, because I do not wish to be alone. Society exists by chemical affinity, and not otherwise.

8 Put any company of people together with freedom for conversation, and a rapid self-distribution takes place, into sets and pairs. The best are accused of exclusiveness. It would be more true to say, they separate as oil from water, as children from old people, without love or hatred in the matter, each seeking his like; and any interference with the affinities would produce constraint and suffocation. All conversation is a magnetic experiment. I know that my friend can talk eloquently; you know that he cannot articulate a sentence: we have seen him in different company. Assort your party, or invite none. Put Stubbs and Coleridge, Quintilian and Aunt Miriam, into pairs, and you make them all wretched. 'Tis an extempore Sing-Sing built in a parlor. Leave them to seek their own mates, and they will be as merry as sparrows.

9 A higher civility will re-establish in our customs a certain reverence which we have lost. What to do with these brisk young men who break through all fences, and make themselves at home in every house? I find out in an instant if my companion does not want me, and ropes cannot hold me when my

3. **mendicant** a beggar
4. **Bacon** an English philosopher and statesman who is credited with developing the scientific method

NOTES

welcome is gone. One would think that the affinities would pronounce themselves with a surer reciprocity.

10 Here again, as so often, Nature delights to put us between extreme antagonisms, and our safety is in the skill with which we keep the diagonal line. Solitude is impracticable, and society fatal. We must keep our head in the one and our hands in the other. The conditions are met, if we keep our independence, yet do not lose our sympathy. These wonderful horses need to be driven by fine hands. We require such a solitude as shall hold us to its revelations when we are in the street and in palaces; for most men are cowed in society, and say good things to you in private, but will not stand to them in public. But let us not be the victims of words. Society and solitude are deceptive names. It is not the circumstance of seeing more or fewer people, but the readiness of sympathy, that imports; and a sound mind will **derive** its principles from insight, with ever a purer ascent to the sufficient and absolute right, and will accept society as the natural element in which they are to be applied.

WRITE

PERSONAL RESPONSE: Emerson expresses the idea that one must attain both solitude and society in life. How does this relate to your own life? In what ways do you thrive in solitude, and in what ways do you thrive in the company of others? Write a reflection about the role of solitude and the role of companionship in your life, responding to specific quotations from the excerpt of Emerson's essay "Society and Solitude."

Walden

ARGUMENTATIVE TEXT
Henry David Thoreau
1854

Introduction

Henry David Thoreau (1817–1862) was a prominent Transcendentalist writer and philosopher from the 19th century. He spent two years in solitude on Walden Pond to escape the chaos and distractions of civilization and his busy life. There, Thoreau observed nature and called himself an "inspector of snow-storms and rainstorms." Thoreau's goal was to live simply and self-sufficiently. In this excerpt from the second chapter of *Walden*, Thoreau explains "Where I Lived and What I Lived For." This text is accompanied by the 1849 oil-on-canvas painting *Kindred Spirits* by the New York artist Asher B. Durand.

"Why should we live with such hurry and waste of life?"

NOTES

Kindred Spirits by Asher B. Durand, 1849

1 I went to the woods because I wished to live deliberately, to front only the essential facts of life, and see if I could not learn what it had to teach, and not, when I came to die, discover that I had not lived. I did not wish to live what was not life, living is so dear; nor did I wish to practise resignation, unless it was quite necessary. I wanted to live deep and suck out all the marrow of life, to live so sturdily and Spartan-like[1] as to put to rout all that was not life, to cut a broad swath and shave close, to drive life into a corner, and reduce it to its lowest terms, and, if it proved to be mean, why then to get the whole and genuine meanness of it, and publish its meanness to the world; or if it were sublime, to know it by experience, and be able to give a true account of it in my next **excursion**. For most men, it appears to me, are in a strange uncertainty about it, whether it is of the devil or of God, and have *somewhat hastily* concluded that it is the chief end of man here to "glorify God and enjoy him forever."

2 Still we live meanly, like ants; though the fable tells us that we were long ago changed into men; like pygmies[2] we fight with cranes; it is error upon error, and clout upon clout, and our best virtue has for its occasion a superfluous and **evitable** wretchedness. Our life is frittered away by detail. An honest man has hardly need to count more than his ten fingers, or in extreme cases he may add his ten toes, and lump the rest. Simplicity, simplicity, simplicity! I say, let your affairs be as two or three, and not a hundred or a thousand; instead of a million count half a dozen, and keep your accounts on your thumb-nail. In the midst of this chopping sea of civilized life, such are the clouds and storms and quicksands and thousand-and-one items to be

1. **Spartan-like** uncaring toward comfort or luxury, as exemplified by ancient Sparta
2. **pygmies** referring to tribal ethnic groups whose average height is especially short

NOTES

allowed for, that a man has to live, if he would not **founder** and go to the bottom and not make his port at all, by dead reckoning, and he must be a great calculator indeed who succeeds. Simplify, simplify. Instead of three meals a day, if it be necessary eat but one; instead of a hundred dishes, five; and reduce other things in proportion. Our life is like a German Confederacy, made up of petty states, with its boundary forever fluctuating, so that even a German cannot tell you how it is bounded at any moment. The nation itself, with all its so-called internal improvements, which, by the way are all external and superficial, is just such an unwieldy and overgrown establishment, cluttered with furniture and tripped up by its own traps, ruined by luxury and heedless expense, by want of calculation and a worthy aim, as the million households in the land; and the only cure for it, as for them, is in a rigid economy, a stern and more than Spartan simplicity of life and elevation of purpose. It lives too fast. Men think that it is essential that the Nation have commerce, and export ice, and talk through a telegraph, and ride thirty miles an hour, without a doubt, whether they do or not; but whether we should live like baboons or like men, is a little uncertain. If we do not get out sleepers, and forge rails, and devote days and nights to the work, but go to tinkering upon our lives to improve them, who will build railroads? And if railroads are not built, how shall we get to heaven in season? But if we stay at home and mind our business, who will want railroads? We do not ride on the railroad; it rides upon us. Did you ever think what those sleepers are that underlie the railroad? Each one is a man, an Irishman, or a Yankee man. The rails are laid on them, and they are covered with sand, and the cars run smoothly over them. They are sound sleepers, I assure you. And every few years a new lot is laid down and run over; so that, if some have the pleasure of riding on a rail, others have the misfortune to be ridden upon. And when they run over a man that is walking in his sleep, a supernumerary sleeper in the wrong position, and wake him up, they suddenly stop the cars, and make a hue and cry about it, as if this were an exception. I am glad to know that it takes a gang of men for every five miles to keep the sleepers down and level in their beds as it is, for this is a sign that they may sometime get up again.

3 Why should we live with such hurry and waste of life? We are determined to be starved before we are hungry. Men say that a stitch in time saves nine, and so they take a thousand stitches today to save nine tomorrow. As for work, we haven't any of any **consequence**. We have the Saint Vitus' dance,[3] and cannot possibly keep our heads still. If I should only give a few pulls at the parish bell-rope, as for a fire, that is, without setting the bell, there is hardly a man on his farm in the outskirts of Concord, notwithstanding that press of engagements which was his excuse so many times this morning, nor a boy, nor a woman, I might almost say, but would forsake all and follow that sound, not mainly to save property from the flames, but,

3. **Saint Vitus' dance** layman's term for Sydenham's chorea, a disorder marked by uncontrolled movements in the head, face, and limbs

NOTES

if we will confess the truth, much more to see it burn, since burn it must, and we, be it known, did not set it on fire—or to see it put out, and have a hand in it, if that is done as handsomely; yes, even if it were the parish church itself. Hardly a man takes a half-hour's nap after dinner, but when he wakes he holds up his head and asks, "What's the news?" as if the rest of mankind had stood his sentinels. Some give directions to be waked every half-hour, doubtless for no other purpose; and then, to pay for it, they tell what they have dreamed. After a night's sleep the news is as indispensable as the breakfast. "Pray tell me anything new that has happened to a man anywhere on this globe"—and he reads it over his coffee and rolls, that a man has had his eyes gouged out this morning on the Wachito River; never dreaming the while that he lives in the dark unfathomed mammoth cave of this world, and has but the **rudiment** of an eye himself.

WRITE

PERSONAL RESPONSE: Thoreau writes that "I went to the woods because I wished to live deliberately." He then goes on to describe what living deliberately means to him—a life away from society and the establishment. After reading this excerpt, do you agree or disagree with his philosophy? Using evidence from the text, as well as your own experiences, write a personal essay in which you explain how you "live deliberately."

Bartleby, the Scrivener: A Story of Wall Street

FICTION
Herman Melville
1853

Introduction

Herman Melville (1819–1891) is best remembered for writing *Moby-Dick*, one of the great American novels, though he also wrote other novels and dozens of short stories and poems. In “Bartleby, the Scrivener: A Story of Wall-Street,” our narrator is an aging lawyer who hires a talented copyist named Bartleby to work in his office as a legal clerk. Although Bartleby’s hard work initially impresses his new employer, his unusual behavior soon extends beyond the limits of what the narrator can tolerate. Melville’s story about depression and isolation in American work culture endures as a classic piece of short fiction. Though Melville’s work was largely ignored during his lifetime, the centennial of his birth in 1919 revived critical interest.

"Ah Bartleby! Ah humanity!"

NOTES

Engraving of a scene outside the New York Stock Exchange at the corner of Wall Street and Broad Street in downtown Manhattan, New York, New York, 1860s (Photo by FPG/ Getty Images)

1 I AM A rather elderly man. The nature of my avocations for the last thirty years has brought me into more than ordinary contact with what would seem an interesting and somewhat singular set of men, of whom as yet nothing that I know of has ever been written:—I mean the law-copyists or scriveners.[1] I have known very many of them, professionally and privately, and if I pleased, could relate divers histories, at which good-natured gentlemen might smile, and sentimental souls might weep. But I waive the biographies of all other scriveners for a few passages in the life of Bartleby, who was a scrivener of the strangest I ever saw or heard of. While of other law-copyists I might write the complete life, of Bartleby nothing of that sort can be done. I believe that no materials exist for a full and satisfactory biography of this man. It is an irreparable loss to literature. Bartleby was one of those beings of whom nothing is ascertainable, except from the original sources, and in his case those are very small. What my own astonished eyes saw of Bartleby, *that* is all I know of him, except, indeed, one vague report which will appear in the sequel.

2 Ere introducing the scrivener, as he first appeared to me, it is fit I make some mention of myself, my *employees*, my business, my chambers, and general surroundings; because some such description is indispensable to an adequate understanding of the chief character about to be presented.

3 Imprimis:[2] I am a man who, from his youth upwards, has been filled with a profound conviction that the easiest way of life is the best. Hence, though I belong to a profession proverbially energetic and nervous, even to turbulence,

1. **law-copyists or scriveners** employees in a law office whose primary job was document production and reproduction
2. **Imprimis** an adverb used to introduce a list of things to think about

NOTES

at times, yet nothing of that sort have I ever suffered to invade my peace. I am one of those unambitious lawyers who never addresses a jury, or in any way draws down public applause; but in the cool tranquillity of a snug retreat, do a snug business among rich men's bonds and mortgages and title-deeds. All who know me, consider me an eminently *safe* man. The late John Jacob Astor,[3] a personage little given to poetic enthusiasm, had no hesitation in pronouncing my first grand point to be prudence; my next, method. I do not speak it in vanity, but simply record the fact, that I was not unemployed in my profession by the late John Jacob Astor; a name which, I admit, I love to repeat, for it hath a rounded and orbicular sound to it, and rings like unto bullion. I will freely add, that I was not insensible to the late John Jacob Astor's good opinion.

4 Some time prior to the period at which this little history begins, my avocations had been largely increased. The good old office, now extinct in the State of New York, of a Master in Chancery, had been conferred upon me. It was not a very arduous office, but very pleasantly remunerative. I seldom lose my temper; much more seldom indulge in dangerous indignation at wrongs and outrages; but I must be permitted to be rash here and declare, that I consider the sudden and violent abrogation of the office of Master in Chancery, by the new Constitution, as a—premature act; inasmuch as I had counted upon a life-lease of the profits, whereas I only received those of a few short years. But this is by the way.

5 My chambers were up stairs at No.—Wall-street. At one end they looked upon the white wall of the interior of a spacious sky-light shaft, penetrating the building from top to bottom. This view might have been considered rather tame than otherwise, deficient in what landscape painters call "life." But if so, the view from the other end of my chambers offered, at least, a contrast, if nothing more. In that direction my windows commanded an unobstructed view of a lofty brick wall, black by age and everlasting shade; which wall required no spy-glass to bring out its lurking beauties, but for the benefit of all near-sighted spectators, was pushed up to within ten feet of my window panes. Owing to the great height of the surrounding buildings, and my chambers being on the second floor, the interval between this wall and mine not a little resembled a huge square cistern.

6 At the period just preceding the advent of Bartleby, I had two persons as copyists in my employment, and a promising lad as an office-boy. First, Turkey; second, Nippers; third, Ginger Nut. These may seem names, the like of which are not usually found in the Directory. In truth they were nicknames, mutually conferred upon each other by my three clerks, and were deemed expressive of their respective persons or characters. Turkey was a short, pursy Englishman of about my own age, that is, somewhere not far from sixty. In the morning,

3. **John Jacob Astor** a prominent American businessman

NOTES

Skill: Point of View

The narrator compares Turkey's face to a brightly burning Christmas fire and the daily route of the sun. He's using exaggeration to make fun of Turkey's anger as just habit and doesn't take it seriously. This is an example of satire.

one might say, his face was of a fine florid hue, but after twelve o'clock, meridian—his dinner hour—it blazed like a grate full of Christmas coals; and continued blazing—but, as it were, with a gradual wane—till 6 o'clock, P.M. or thereabouts, after which I saw no more of the proprietor of the face, which gaining its meridian with the sun, seemed to set with it, to rise, culminate, and decline the following day, with the like regularity and undiminished glory. There are many singular coincidences I have known in the course of my life, not the least among which was the fact, that exactly when Turkey displayed his fullest beams from his red and radiant countenance, just then, too, at that critical moment, began the daily period when I considered his business capacities as seriously disturbed for the remainder of the twenty-four hours. Not that he was absolutely idle, or averse to business then; far from it. The difficulty was, he was apt to be altogether too energetic. There was a strange, inflamed, flurried, flighty recklessness of activity about him. He would be incautious in dipping his pen into his inkstand. All his blots upon my documents, were dropped there after twelve o'clock, meridian. Indeed, not only would he be reckless and sadly given to making blots in the afternoon, but some days he went further, and was rather noisy. At such times, too, his face flamed with augmented blazonry, as if cannel coal had been heaped on anthracite. He made an unpleasant racket with his chair; spilled his sand-box; in mending his pens, impatiently split them all to pieces, and threw them on the floor in a sudden passion; stood up and leaned over his table, boxing his papers about in a most indecorous manner, very sad to behold in an elderly man like him. Nevertheless, as he was in many ways a most valuable person to me, and all the time before twelve o'clock, meridian, was the quickest, steadiest creature too, accomplishing a great deal of work in a style not easy to be matched—for these reasons, I was willing to overlook his eccentricities, though indeed, occasionally, I remonstrated with him. I did this very gently, however, because, though the civilest, nay, the blandest and most reverential of men in the morning, yet in the afternoon he was disposed, upon provocation, to be slightly rash with his tongue, in fact, insolent. Now, valuing his morning services as I did, and resolved not to lose them; yet, at the same time made uncomfortable by his inflamed ways after twelve o'clock; and being a man of peace, unwilling by my admonitions to call forth unseemly retorts from him; I took upon me, one Saturday noon (he was always worse on Saturdays), to hint to him, very kindly, that perhaps now that he was growing old, it might be well to **abridge** his labors; in short, he need not come to my chambers after twelve o'clock, but, dinner over, had best go home to his lodgings and rest himself till teatime. But no; he insisted upon his afternoon devotions. His countenance became intolerably fervid, as he oratorically assured me—gesticulating with a long ruler at the other end of the room—that if his services in the morning were useful, how indispensable, then, in the afternoon?

7 "With submission, sir," said Turkey on this occasion, "I consider myself your right-hand man. In the morning I but marshal and deploy my columns; but in

NOTES

the afternoon I put myself at their head, and gallantly charge the foe, thus!"—and he made a violent thrust with the ruler.

8 "But the blots, Turkey," intimated I.

9 "True,—but, with submission, sir, behold these hairs! I am getting old. Surely, sir, a blot or two of a warm afternoon is not to be severely urged against gray hairs. Old age—even if it blot the page—is honorable. With submission, sir, we *both* are getting old."

10 This appeal to my fellow-feeling was hardly to be resisted. At all events, I saw that go he would not. So I made up my mind to let him stay, resolving, nevertheless, to see to it, that during the afternoon he had to do with my less important papers.

11 Nippers, the second on my list, was a whiskered, sallow, and, upon the whole, rather piratical-looking young man of about five and twenty. I always deemed him the victim of two evil powers—ambition and indigestion. The ambition was evinced by a certain impatience of the duties of a mere copyist, an unwarrantable usurpation of strictly professional affairs, such as the original drawing up of legal documents. The indigestion seemed betokened in an occasional nervous testiness and grinning irritability, causing the teeth to audibly grind together over mistakes committed in copying; unnecessary maledictions, hissed, rather than spoken, in the heat of business; and especially by a continual discontent with the height of the table where he worked. Though of a very ingenious mechanical turn, Nippers could never get this table to suit him. He put chips under it, blocks of various sorts, bits of pasteboard, and at last went so far as to attempt an exquisite adjustment by final pieces of folded blotting paper. But no invention would answer. If, for the sake of easing his back, he brought the table lid at a sharp angle well up towards his chin, and wrote there like a man using the steep roof of a Dutch house for his desk:—then he declared that it stopped the circulation in his arms. If now he lowered the table to his waistbands, and stooped over it in writing, then there was a sore aching in his back. In short, the truth of the matter was, Nippers knew not what he wanted. Or, if he wanted any thing, it was to be rid of a scrivener's table altogether. Among the manifestations of his diseased ambition was a fondness he had for receiving visits from certain ambiguous-looking fellows in seedy coats, whom he called his clients. Indeed I was aware that not only was he, at times, considerable of a ward-politician, but he occasionally did a little business at the Justices' courts, and was not unknown on the steps of the Tombs. I have good reason to believe, however, that one individual who called upon him at my chambers, and who, with a grand air, he insisted was his client, was no other than a dun, and the alleged title-deed, a bill. But with all his failings, and the annoyances he caused me, Nippers, like his compatriot Turkey, was a very useful man to me; wrote a neat, swift hand; and, when he chose, was not deficient in a gentlemanly sort

NOTES

of deportment. Added to this, he always dressed in a gentlemanly sort of way; and so, incidentally, reflected credit upon my chambers. Whereas with respect to Turkey, I had much ado to keep him from being a reproach to me. His clothes were apt to look oily and smell of eating-houses. He wore his pantaloons very loose and baggy in summer. His coats were execrable; his hat not to be handled. But while the hat was a thing of indifference to me, inasmuch as his natural civility and deference, as a dependent Englishman, always led him to doff it the moment he entered the room, yet his coat was another matter. Concerning his coats, I reasoned with him; but with no effect. The truth was, I suppose, that a man of so small an income, could not afford to sport such a lustrous face and a lustrous coat at one and the same time. As Nippers once observed, Turkey's money went chiefly for red ink. One winter day I presented Turkey with a highly-respectable looking coat of my own, a padded gray coat, of a most comfortable warmth, and which buttoned straight up from the knee to the neck. I thought Turkey would appreciate the favor, and abate his rashness and obstreperousness of afternoons. But no. I verily believe that buttoning himself up in so downy and blanket-like a coat had a pernicious effect upon him; upon the same principle that too much oats are bad for horses. In fact, precisely as a rash, restive horse is said to feel his oats, so Turkey felt his coat. It made him insolent. He was a man whom prosperity harmed.

12 Though concerning the self-indulgent habits of Turkey I had my own private surmises, yet touching Nippers I was well persuaded that whatever might by his faults in other respects, he was, at least, a temperate young man. But indeed, nature herself seemed to have been his vintner, and at his birth charged him so thoroughly with an irritable, brandy-like disposition, that all subsequent potations were needless. When I consider how, amid the stillness of my chambers, Nippers would sometimes impatiently rise from his seat, and stooping over his table, spread his arms wide apart, seize the whole desk, and move it, and jerk it, with a grim, grinding motion on the floor, as if the table were a perverse voluntary agent, intent on thwarting and vexing him; I plainly perceive that for Nippers, brandy and water were altogether superfluous.

13 It was fortunate for me that, owing to its peculiar cause—indigestion— the irritability and consequent nervousness of Nippers, were mainly observable in the morning, while in the afternoon he was comparatively mild. So that Turkey's paroxysms only coming on about twelve o'clock, I never had to do with their eccentricities at one time. Their fits relieved each other like guards. When Nippers' was on, Turkey's was off; and *vice versa*. This was a good natural arrangement under the circumstances.

14 Ginger Nut, the third on my list, was a lad some twelve years old. His father was a carman, ambitious of seeing his son on the bench instead of a cart, before he died. So he sent him to my office as student at law, errand boy, and cleaner and sweeper, at the rate of one dollar a week. He had a little desk to

himself, but he did not use it much. Upon inspection, the drawer exhibited a great array of the shells of various sorts of nuts. Indeed, to this quick-witted youth the whole noble science of the law was contained in a nut-shell. Not the least among the employments of Ginger Nut, as well as one which he discharged with the most **alacrity**, was his duty as cake and apple purveyor for Turkey and Nippers. Copying law papers being proverbially dry, husky sort of business, my two scriveners were fain to moisten their mouths very often with Spitzenbergs to be had at the numerous stalls nigh the Custom House and Post Office. Also, they sent Ginger Nut very frequently for that peculiar cake—small, flat, round, and very spicy—after which he had been named by them. Of a cold morning when business was but dull, Turkey would gobble up scores of these cakes, as if they were mere wafers—indeed they sell them at the rate of six or eight for a penny—the scrape of his pen blending with the crunching of the crisp particles in his mouth. Of all the fiery afternoon blunders and flurried rashnesses of Turkey, was his once moistening a ginger-cake between his lips, and clapping it on to a mortgage for a seal. I came within an ace of dismissing him then. But he mollified me by making an oriental bow, and saying—"With submission, sir, it was generous of me to find you in stationery on my own account."

15 Now my original business—that of a conveyancer and title hunter, and drawer-up of recondite documents of all sorts—was considerably increased by receiving the master's office. There was now great work for scriveners. Not only must I push the clerks already with me, but I must have additional help. In answer to my advertisement, a motionless young man one morning, stood upon my office threshold, the door being open, for it was summer. I can see that figure now—pallidly neat, pitiably respectable, incurably forlorn! It was Bartleby.

16 After a few words touching his qualifications, I engaged him, glad to have among my corps of copyists a man of so singularly sedate an aspect, which I thought might operate beneficially upon the flighty temper of Turkey, and the fiery one of Nippers.

17 I should have stated before that ground glass folding-doors divided my premises into two parts, one of which was occupied by my scriveners, the other by myself. According to my humor I threw open these doors, or closed them. I resolved to assign Bartleby a corner by the folding-doors, but on my side of them, so as to have this quiet man within easy call, in case any trifling thing was to be done. I placed his desk close up to a small side-window in that part of the room, a window which originally had afforded a lateral view of certain grimy back-yards and bricks, but which, owing to subsequent erections, commanded at present no view at all, though it gave some light. Within three feet of the panes was a wall, and the light came down from far above, between two lofty buildings, as from a very small opening in a dome. Still further to a satisfactory arrangement, I procured a high green folding

NOTES

Skill: Theme

The narrator meets a pale, "forlorn" young applicant who just stands "motionless" at the office door. This description reminds me of loneliness and isolation and makes me wonder if one of the themes may relate to loneliness.

NOTES

screen, which might entirely isolate Bartleby from my sight, though not remove him from my voice. And thus, in a manner, privacy and society were conjoined.

18 At first Bartleby did an extraordinary quantity of writing. As if long famishing for something to copy, he seemed to gorge himself on my documents. There was no pause for digestion. He ran a day and night line, copying by sun-light and by candle-light. I should have been quite delighted with his application, had he been cheerfully industrious. But he wrote on silently, palely, mechanically.

Skill: Figurative Language

This passage uses hyperbole to emphasize Bartleby's work habits. The hyperbole seems to suggest that the narrator finds Bartleby's behavior strange and off-putting.

19 It is, of course, an indispensable part of a scrivener's business to verify the accuracy of his copy, word by word. Where there are two or more scriveners in an office, they assist each other in this examination, one reading from the copy, the other holding the original. It is a very dull, wearisome, and **lethargic** affair. I can readily imagine that to some sanguine temperaments it would be altogether intolerable. For example, I cannot credit that the mettlesome poet Byron would have contentedly sat down with Bartleby to examine a law document of, say five hundred pages, closely written in a crimpy hand.

20 Now and then, in the haste of business, it had been my habit to assist in comparing some brief document myself, calling Turkey or Nippers for this purpose. One object I had in placing Bartleby so handy to me behind the screen, was to avail myself of his services on such trivial occasions. It was on the third day, I think, of his being with me, and before any necessity had arisen for having his own writing examined, that, being much hurried to complete a small affair I had in hand, I abruptly called to Bartleby. In my haste and natural expectancy of instant compliance, I sat with my head bent over the original on my desk, and my right hand sideways, and somewhat nervously extended with the copy, so that immediately upon emerging from his retreat, Bartleby might snatch it and proceed to business without the least delay.

Skill: Figurative Language

The description of Bartleby as having a "mild, firm voice" is paradoxical. These two adjectives seem to contradict each other, emphasizing the idea that Bartleby is very peculiar.

21 In this very attitude did I sit when I called to him, rapidly stating what it was I wanted him to do—namely, to examine a small paper with me. Imagine my surprise, nay, my consternation, when without moving from his privacy, Bartleby in a singularly mild, firm voice, replied, "I would prefer not to."

22 I sat awhile in perfect silence, rallying my stunned faculties. Immediately it occurred to me that my ears had deceived me, or Bartleby had entirely misunderstood my meaning. I repeated my request in the clearest tone I could assume. But in quite as clear a one came the previous reply, "I would prefer not to."

23 "Prefer not to," echoed I, rising in high excitement, and crossing the room with a stride. "What do you mean? Are you moon-struck? I want you to help me compare this sheet here—take it," and I thrust it towards him.

NOTES

24 “I would prefer not to,” said he.

25 I looked at him steadfastly. His face was leanly composed; his gray eye dimly calm. Not a wrinkle of agitation rippled him. Had there been the least uneasiness, anger, impatience or impertinence in his manner; in other words, had there been any thing ordinarily human about him, doubtless I should have violently dismissed him from the premises. But as it was, I should have as soon thought of turning my pale plaster-of-paris bust of Cicero out of doors. I stood gazing at him awhile, as he went on with his own writing, and then reseated myself at my desk. This is very strange, thought I. What had one best do? But my business hurried me. I concluded to forget the matter for the present, reserving it for my future leisure. So calling Nippers from the other room, the paper was speedily examined.

26 A few days after this, Bartleby concluded four lengthy documents, being quadruplicates of a week's testimony taken before me in my High Court of Chancery. It became necessary to examine them. It was an important suit, and great accuracy was imperative. Having all things arranged I called Turkey, Nippers and Ginger Nut from the next room, meaning to place the four copies in the hands of my four clerks, while I should read from the original. Accordingly Turkey, Nippers and Ginger Nut had taken their seats in a row, each with his document in hand, when I called to Bartleby to join this interesting group.

27 “Bartleby! quick, I am waiting.”

28 I heard a slow scrape of his chair legs on the uncarpeted floor, and soon he appeared standing at the entrance of his hermitage.

29 “What is wanted?” said he mildly.

30 “The copies, the copies,” said I hurriedly. “We are going to examine them. There”—and I held towards him the fourth quadruplicate.

31 “I would prefer not to,” he said, and gently disappeared behind the screen.

32 For a few moments I was turned into a pillar of salt,[4] standing at the head of my seated column of clerks. Recovering myself, I advanced towards the screen, and demanded the reason for such extraordinary conduct.

33 “*Why* do you refuse?”

34 “I would prefer not to.”

35 With any other man I should have flown outright into a dreadful passion, scorned all further words, and thrust him ignominiously from my presence. But there was something about Bartleby that not only strangely disarmed me,

Skill: Theme

Bartleby's repetition of the phrase “I would prefer not to” makes me think. It brings out the idea of passive resistance—refusing to conform to social norms. Is passive resistance another theme?

4. **pillar of salt** In the Bible, Lot's wife was turned into a pillar of salt when she disobeyed God's command not to look back at the destruction of Sodom and Gomorrah.

NOTES

but in a wonderful manner touched and disconcerted me. I began to reason with him.

36 "These are your own copies we are about to examine. It is labor saving to you, because one examination will answer for your four papers. It is common usage. Every copyist is bound to help examine his copy. Is it not so? Will you not speak? Answer!"

37 "I prefer not to," he replied in a flute-like tone. It seemed to me that while I had been addressing him, he carefully revolved every statement that I made; fully comprehended the meaning; could not gainsay the irresistible conclusions; but, at the same time, some paramount consideration prevailed with him to reply as he did.

38 "You are decided, then, not to comply with my request—a request made according to common usage and common sense?"

39 He briefly gave me to understand that on that point my judgment was sound. Yes: his decision was irreversible.

40 It is not seldom the case that when a man is browbeaten in some unprecedented and violently unreasonable way, he begins to stagger in his own plainest faith. He begins, as it were, vaguely to surmise that, wonderful as it may be, all the justice and all the reason is on the other side. Accordingly, if any disinterested persons are present, he turns to them for some reinforcement for his own faltering mind.

41 "Turkey," said I, "what do you think of this? Am I not right?"

42 "With submission, sir," said Turkey, with his blandest tone, "I think that you are."

43 "Nippers," said I, "what do *you* think of it?"

44 "I think I should kick him out of the office."

45 (The reader of nice perceptions will here perceive that, it being morning, Turkey's answer is couched in polite and tranquil terms, but Nippers replies in ill-tempered ones. Or, to repeat a previous sentence, Nippers' ugly mood was on duty and Turkey's off.)

46 "Ginger Nut," said I, willing to enlist the smallest suffrage in my behalf, "what do *you* think of it?"

47 "I think, sir, he's a little *luny*," replied Ginger Nut with a grin.

48 "You hear what they say," said I, turning towards the screen, "come forth and do your duty."

NOTES

49 But he vouchsafed no reply. I pondered a moment in sore perplexity. But once more business hurried me. I determined again to postpone the consideration of this dilemma to my future leisure. With a little trouble we made out to examine the papers without Bartleby, though at every page or two, Turkey deferentially dropped his opinion that this proceeding was quite out of the common; while Nippers, twitching in his chair with a dyspeptic nervousness, ground out between his set teeth occasional hissing maledictions against the stubborn oaf behind the screen. And for his (Nippers') part, this was the first and the last time he would do another man's business without pay.

50 Meanwhile Bartleby sat in his hermitage, oblivious to every thing but his own peculiar business there.

51 Some days passed, the scrivener being employed upon another lengthy work. His late remarkable conduct led me to regard his ways narrowly. I observed that he never went to dinner; indeed that he never went any where. As yet I had never of my personal knowledge known him to be outside of my office. He was a perpetual sentry in the corner. At about eleven o'clock though, in the morning, I noticed that Ginger Nut would advance toward the opening in Bartleby's screen, as if silently beckoned thither by a gesture invisible to me where I sat. The boy would then leave the office jingling a few pence, and reappear with a handful of ginger-nuts which he delivered in the hermitage, receiving two of the cakes for his trouble.

52 He lives, then, on ginger-nuts, thought I; never eats a dinner, properly speaking; he must be a vegetarian then; but no; he never eats even vegetables, he eats nothing but ginger-nuts. My mind then ran on in reveries concerning the probable effects upon the human constitution of living entirely on ginger-nuts. Ginger-nuts are so called because they contain ginger as one of their peculiar constituents, and the final flavoring one. Now what was ginger? A hot, spicy thing. Was Bartleby hot and spicy? Not at all. Ginger, then, had no effect upon Bartleby. Probably he preferred it should have none.

53 Nothing so aggravates an earnest person as a passive resistance. If the individual so resisted be of a not inhumane temper, and the resisting one perfectly harmless in his passivity; then, in the better moods of the former, he will endeavor charitably to construe to his imagination what proves impossible to be solved by his judgment. Even so, for the most part, I regarded Bartleby and his ways. Poor fellow! Thought I, he means no mischief; it is plain he intends no insolence; his aspect sufficiently evinces that his eccentricities are involuntary. He is useful to me. I can get along with him. If I turn him away, the chances are he will fall in with some less indulgent employer, and then he will be rudely treated, and perhaps driven forth miserably to starve. Yes. Here I can cheaply purchase a delicious self-approval. To befriend Bartleby; to humor him in his strange willfulness, will cost me little or nothing, while I lay

NOTES

up in my soul what will eventually prove a sweet morsel for my conscience. But this mood was not invariable with me. The passiveness of Bartleby sometimes irritated me. I felt strangely goaded on to encounter him in new opposition, to elicit some angry spark from him answerable to my own. But indeed I might as well have essayed to strike fire with my knuckles against a bit of Windsor soap. But one afternoon the evil impulse in me mastered me, and the following little scene ensued:

54 "Bartleby," said I, "when those papers are all copied, I will compare them with you."

55 "I would prefer not to."

56 "How? Surely you do not mean to persist in that mulish vagary?"

57 No answer.

58 I threw open the folding-doors near by, and turning upon Turkey and Nippers, exclaimed in an excited manner—

59 "He says, a second time, he won't examine his papers. What do you think of it, Turkey?"

60 It was afternoon, be it remembered. Turkey sat glowing like a brass boiler, his bald head steaming, his hands reeling among his blotted papers.

61 "Think of it?" roared Turkey; "I think I'll just step behind his screen, and black his eyes for him!"

62 So saying, Turkey rose to his feet and threw his arms into a pugilistic position. He was hurrying away to make good his promise, when I detained him, alarmed at the effect of incautiously rousing Turkey's combativeness after dinner.

63 "Sit down, Turkey," said I, "and hear what Nippers has to say. What do you think of it, Nippers? Would I not be justified in immediately dismissing Bartleby?"

64 "Excuse me, that is for you to decide, sir. I think his conduct quite unusual, and indeed unjust, as regards Turkey and myself. But it may only be a passing whim."

65 "Ah," exclaimed I, "you have strangely changed your mind then—you speak very gently of him now."

66 "All beer," cried Turkey; "gentleness is effects of beer—Nippers and I dined together to-day. You see how gentle *I* am, sir. Shall I go and black his eyes?"

67 "You refer to Bartleby, I suppose. No, not to-day, Turkey," I replied; "pray, put up your fists."

NOTES

68 I closed the doors, and again advanced towards Bartleby. I felt additional incentives tempting me to my fate. I burned to be rebelled against again. I remembered that Bartleby never left the office.

69 "Bartleby," said I, "Ginger Nut is away; just step round to the Post Office, won't you? (it was but a three-minute walk,) and see if there is any thing for me."

70 "I would prefer not to."

71 "You *will* not?"

72 "I *prefer* not."

73 I staggered to my desk, and sat there in a deep study. My blind inveteracy returned. Was there any other thing in which I could procure myself to be ignominiously repulsed by this lean, penniless wight?—my hired clerk? What added thing is there, perfectly reasonable, that he will be sure to refuse to do?

74 "Bartleby!"

75 No answer.

76 "Bartleby," in a louder tone.

77 No answer.

78 "Bartleby," I roared.

79 Like a very ghost, agreeably to the laws of magical invocation, at the third summons, he appeared at the entrance of his hermitage.

80 "Go to the next room, and tell Nippers to come to me."

81 "I prefer not to," he respectfully and slowly said, and mildly disappeared.

82 "Very good, Bartleby," said I, in a quiet sort of serenely severe self-possessed tone, intimating the unalterable purpose of some terrible retribution very close at hand. At the moment I half intended something of the kind. But upon the whole, as it was drawing towards my dinner-hour, I thought it best to put on my hat and walk home for the day, suffering much from perplexity and distress of mind.

83 Shall I acknowledge it? The conclusion of this whole business was, that it soon became a fixed fact of my chambers, that a pale young scrivener, by the name of Bartleby, had a desk there; that he copied for me at the usual rate of four cents a folio (one hundred words); but he was permanently exempt from examining the work done by him, that duty being transferred to Turkey and Nippers, one of compliment doubtless to their superior acuteness; moreover, said Bartleby was never on any account to be dispatched on the most trivial

NOTES

errand of any sort; and that even if entreated to take upon him such a matter, it was generally understood that he would prefer not to—in other words, that he would refuse point-blank.

84 As days passed on, I became considerably reconciled to Bartleby. His steadiness, his freedom from all dissipation, his incessant industry (except when he chose to throw himself into a standing revery behind his screen), his great stillness, his unalterableness of demeanor under all circumstances, made him a valuable acquisition. One prime thing was this,—*he was always there*;—first in the morning, continually through the day, and the last at night. I had a singular confidence in his honesty. I felt my most precious papers perfectly safe in his hands. Sometimes to be sure I could not, for the very soul of me, avoid falling into sudden spasmodic passions with him. For it was exceeding difficult to bear in mind all the time those strange peculiarities, privileges, and unheard of exemptions, forming the tacit stipulations on Bartleby's part under which he remained in my office. Now and then, in the eagerness of dispatching pressing business, I would inadvertently summon Bartleby, in a short, rapid tone, to put his finger, say, on the incipient tie of a bit of red tape with which I was about compressing some papers. Of course, from behind the screen the usual answer, "I prefer not to," was sure to come; and then, how could a human creature with the common infirmities of our nature, refrain from bitterly exclaiming upon such perverseness—such unreasonableness. However, every added repulse of this sort which I received only tended to lessen the probability of my repeating the inadvertence.

85 Here it must be said, that according to the custom of most legal gentlemen occupying chambers in densely-populated law buildings, there were several keys to my door. One was kept by a woman residing in the attic, which person weekly scrubbed and daily swept and dusted my apartments. Another was kept by Turkey for convenience sake. The third I sometimes carried in my own pocket. The fourth I knew not who had.

86 Now, one Sunday morning I happened to go to Trinity Church, to hear a celebrated preacher, and finding myself rather early on the ground, I thought I would walk around to my chambers for a while. Luckily I had my key with me; but upon applying it to the lock, I found it resisted by something inserted from the inside. Quite surprised, I called out; when to my consternation a key was turned from within; and thrusting his lean visage at me, and holding the door ajar, the apparition of Bartleby appeared, in his shirt sleeves, and otherwise in a strangely tattered dishabille, saying quietly that he was sorry, but he was deeply engaged just then, and—preferred not admitting me at present. In a brief word or two, he moreover added, that perhaps I had better walk round the block two or three times, and by that time he would probably have concluded his affairs.

NOTES

87 Now, the utterly **unsurmised** appearance of Bartleby, tenanting my law-chambers of a Sunday morning, with his cadaverously gentlemanly *nonchalance*, yet withal firm and self-possessed, had such a strange effect upon me, that incontinently I slunk away from my own door, and did as desired. But not without sundry twinges of impotent rebellion against the mild effrontery of this unaccountable scrivener. Indeed, it was his wonderful mildness chiefly, which not only disarmed me, but unmanned me, as it were. For I consider that one, for the time, is a sort of unmanned when he tranquilly permits his hired clerk to dictate to him, and order him away from his own premises. Furthermore, I was full of uneasiness as to what Bartleby could possibly be doing in my office in his shirt sleeves, and in an otherwise dismantled condition of a Sunday morning. Was any thing amiss going on? Nay, that was out of the question. It was not to be thought of for a moment that Bartleby was an immoral person. But what could he be doing there?—copying? Nay again, whatever might be his eccentricities, Bartleby was an eminently decorous person. He would be the last man to sit down to his desk in any state approaching to nudity. Besides, it was Sunday; and there was something about Bartleby that forbade the supposition that he would by any secular occupation violate the proprieties of the day.

88 Nevertheless, my mind was not pacified; and full of a restless curiosity, at last I returned to the door. Without hindrance I inserted my key, opened it, and entered. Bartleby was not to be seen. I looked round anxiously, peeped behind his screen; but it was very plain that he was gone. Upon more closely examining the place, I surmised that for an indefinite period Bartleby must have ate, dressed, and slept in my office, and that too without plate, mirror, or bed. The cushioned seat of a rickety old sofa in one corner bore the faint impress of a lean, reclining form. Rolled away under his desk, I found a blanket; under the empty grate, a blacking box and brush; on a chair, a tin basin, with soap and a ragged towel; in a newspaper a few crumbs of ginger-nuts and a morsel of cheese. Yes, thought I, it is evident enough that Bartleby has been making his home here, keeping bachelor's hall all by himself. Immediately then the thought came sweeping across me, What miserable friendlessness and loneliness are here revealed! His poverty is great; but his solitude, how horrible! Think of it. Of a Sunday, Wall-street is deserted as Petra; and every night of every day it is an emptiness. This building too, which of week-days hums with industry and life, at nightfall echoes with sheer vacancy, and all through Sunday is forlorn. And here Bartleby makes his home; sole spectator of a solitude which he has seen all populous—a sort of innocent and transformed Marius[5] brooding among the ruins of Carthage!

89 For the first time in my life a feeling of overpowering stinging melancholy seized me. Before, I had never experienced aught but a not-unpleasing

5. **Marius** Gaius Marius, a Roman general and statesman, who was exiled to the destroyed city of Carthage

sadness. The bond of a common humanity now drew me irresistibly to gloom. A fraternal melancholy! For both I and Bartleby were sons of Adam. I remembered the bright silks and sparkling faces I had seen that day, in gala trim, swan-like sailing down the Mississippi of Broadway; and I contrasted them with the pallid copyist, and thought to myself, Ah, happiness courts the light, so we deem the world is gay; but misery hides aloof, so we deem that misery there is none. These sad fancyings—chimeras, doubtless, of a sick and silly brain—led on to other and more special thoughts, concerning the eccentricities of Bartleby. Presentiments of strange discoveries hovered round me. The scrivener's pale form appeared to me laid out, among uncaring strangers, in its shivering winding sheet.

90 Suddenly I was attracted by Bartleby's closed desk, the key in open sight left in the lock.

91 I mean no mischief, seek the gratification of no heartless curiosity, thought I; besides, the desk is mine, and its contents too, so I will make bold to look within. Every thing was methodically arranged, the papers smoothly placed. The pigeon holes were deep, and removing the files of documents, I groped into their recesses. Presently I felt something there, and dragged it out. It was an old bandanna handkerchief, heavy and knotted. I opened it, and saw it was a savings' bank.

92 I now recalled all the quiet mysteries which I had noted in the man. I remembered that he never spoke but to answer; that though at intervals he had considerable time to himself, yet I had never seen him reading—no, not even a newspaper; that for long periods he would stand looking out, at his pale window behind the screen, upon the dead brick wall; I was quite sure he never visited any refectory or eating house; while his pale face clearly indicated that he never drank beer like Turkey, or tea and coffee even, like other men; that he never went any where in particular that I could learn; never went out for a walk, unless indeed that was the case at present; that he had declined telling who he was, or whence he came, or whether he had any relatives in the world; that though so thin and pale, he never complained of ill health. And more than all, I remembered a certain unconscious air of pallid—how shall I call it?—of pallid haughtiness, say, or rather an austere reserve about him, which had positively awed me into my tame compliance with his eccentricities, when I had feared to ask him to do the slightest incidental thing for me, even though I might know, from his long-continued motionlessness, that behind his screen he must be standing in one of those dead-wall reveries of his.

93 Revolving all these things, and coupling them with the recently discovered fact that he made my office his constant abiding place and home, and not forgetful of his morbid moodiness; revolving all these things, a prudential feeling began to steal over me. My first emotions had been those of pure

NOTES

melancholy and sincerest pity; but just in proportion as the forlornness of Bartleby grew and grew to my imagination, did that same melancholy merge into fear, that pity into repulsion. So true it is, and so terrible too, that up to a certain point the thought or sight of misery enlists our best affections; but, in certain special cases, beyond that point it does not. They err who would assert that invariably this is owing to the inherent selfishness of the human heart. It rather proceeds from a certain hopelessness of remedying excessive and organic ill. To a sensitive being, pity is not seldom pain. And when at last it is perceived that such pity cannot lead to effectual succor, common sense bids the soul rid of it. What I saw that morning persuaded me that the scrivener was the victim of innate and incurable disorder. I might give alms to his body; but his body did not pain him; it was his soul that suffered, and his soul I could not reach.

94 I did not accomplish the purpose of going to Trinity Church that morning. Somehow, the things I had seen disqualified me for the time from church-going. I walked homeward, thinking what I would do with Bartleby. Finally, I resolved upon this;—I would put certain calm questions to him the next morning, touching his history, etc., and if he declined to answer them openly and unreservedly (and I supposed he would prefer not), then to give him a twenty-dollar bill over and above whatever I might owe him, and tell him his services were no longer required; but that if in any other way I could assist him, I would be happy to do so, especially if he desired to return to his native place, wherever that might be, I would willingly help to defray the expenses. Moreover, if, after reaching home, he found himself at any time in want of aid, a letter from him would be sure of a reply.

95 The next morning came.

96 “Bartleby,” said I, gently calling to him behind his screen.

97 No reply.

98 “Bartleby,” said I, in a still gentler tone, “come here; I am not going to ask you to do any thing you would prefer not to do—I simply wish to speak to you.”

99 Upon this he noiselessly slid into view.

100 “Will you tell me, Bartleby, where you were born?”

101 “I would prefer not to.”

102 “Will you tell me *any thing* about yourself?”

103 “I would prefer not to.”

104 “But what reasonable objection can you have to speak to me? I feel friendly towards you.”

NOTES

105 He did not look at me while I spoke, but kept his glance fixed upon my bust of Cicero, which as I then sat, was directly behind me, some six inches above my head.

106 "What is your answer, Bartleby?" said I, after waiting a considerable time for a reply, during which his countenance remained immovable, only there was the faintest conceivable tremor of the white attenuated mouth.

107 "At present I prefer to give no answer," he said, and retired into his hermitage.

108 It was rather weak in me I confess, but his manner on this occasion nettled me. Not only did there seem to lurk in it a certain calm disdain, but his perverseness seemed ungrateful, considering the undeniable good usage and indulgence he had received from me.

109 Again I sat ruminating what I should do. Mortified as I was at his behavior, and resolved as I had been to dismiss him when I entered my offices, nevertheless I strangely felt something superstitious knocking at my heart, and forbidding me to carry out my purpose, and denouncing me for a villain if I dared to breathe one bitter word against this forlornest of mankind. At last, familiarly drawing my chair behind his screen, I sat down and said: "Bartleby, never mind then about revealing your history; but let me entreat you, as a friend, to comply as far as may be with the usages of this office. Say now you will help to examine papers to-morrow or next day: in short, say now that in a day or two you will begin to be a little reasonable:—say so, Bartleby."

110 "At present I would prefer not to be a little reasonable," was his mildly cadaverous reply. Just then the folding-doors opened, and Nippers approached. He seemed suffering from an unusually bad night's rest, induced by severer indigestion than common. He overheard those final words of Bartleby.

111 "*Prefer not*, eh?" gritted Nippers—"I'd *prefer* him, if I were you, sir," addressing me—"I'd *prefer* him; I'd give him preferences, the stubborn mule! What is it, sir, pray, that he *prefers* not to do now?"

112 Bartleby moved not a limb.

113 "Mr. Nippers," said I, "I'd prefer that you would withdraw for the present."

114 Somehow, of late I had got into the way of involuntarily using this word "prefer" upon all sorts of not exactly suitable occasions. And I trembled to think that my contact with the scrivener had already and seriously affected me in a mental way. And what further and deeper aberration might it not yet produce? This apprehension had not been without efficacy in determining me to summary means.

NOTES

115 As Nippers, looking very sour and sulky, was departing, Turkey blandly and deferentially approached.

116 "With submission, sir," said he, "yesterday I was thinking about Bartleby here, and I think that if he would but prefer to take a quart of good ale every day, it would do much towards mending him, and enabling him to assist in examining his papers."

117 "So you have got the word too," said I, slightly excited.

118 "With submission, what word, sir," asked Turkey, respectfully crowding himself into the contracted space behind the screen, and by so doing, making me jostle the scrivener. "What word, sir?"

119 "I would prefer to be left alone here," said Bartleby, as if offended at being mobbed in his privacy.

120 "*That's* the word, Turkey," said I—"*that's* it." "Oh, *prefer*? oh yes—queer word. I never use it myself. But, sir, as I was saying, if he would but prefer—"

121 "Turkey," interrupted I, "you will please withdraw."

122 "Oh certainly, sir, if you prefer that I should."

123 As he opened the folding-door to retire, Nippers at his desk caught a glimpse of me, and asked whether I would prefer to have a certain paper copied on blue paper or white. He did not in the least roguishly accent the word prefer. It was plain that it involuntarily rolled from his tongue. I thought to myself, surely I must get rid of a demented man, who already has in some degree turned the tongues, if not the heads of myself and clerks. But I thought it **prudent** not to break the dismission at once.

124 The next day I noticed that Bartleby did nothing but stand at his window in his dead-wall revery. Upon asking him why he did not write, he said that he had decided upon doing no more writing.

125 "Why, how now? what next?" exclaimed I, "do no more writing?"

126 "No more."

127 "And what is the reason?"

128 "Do you not see the reason for yourself?" he indifferently replied.

129 I looked steadfastly at him, and perceived that his eyes looked dull and glazed. Instantly it occurred to me, that his unexampled diligence in copying by his dim window for the first few weeks of his stay with me might have temporarily impaired his vision.

NOTES

130 I was touched. I said something in condolence with him. I hinted that of course he did wisely in abstaining from writing for a while; and urged him to embrace that opportunity of taking wholesome exercise in the open air. This, however, he did not do. A few days after this, my other clerks being absent, and being in a great hurry to dispatch certain letters by the mail, I thought that, having nothing else earthly to do, Bartleby would surely be less inflexible than usual, and carry these letters to the post-office. But he blankly declined. So, much to my inconvenience, I went myself.

131 Still added days went by. Whether Bartleby's eyes improved or not, I could not say. To all appearance, I thought they did. But when I asked him if they did, he vouchsafed no answer. At all events, he would do no copying. At last, in reply to my urgings, he informed me that he had permanently given up copying.

132 "What!" exclaimed I; "suppose your eyes should get entirely well—better than ever before—would you not copy then?"

133 "I have given up copying," he answered, and slid aside.

134 He remained as ever, a fixture in my chamber. Nay—if that were possible—he became still more of a fixture than before. What was to be done? He would do nothing in the office: why should he stay there? In plain fact, he had now become a millstone to me, not only useless as a necklace, but afflictive to bear. Yet I was sorry for him. I speak less than truth when I say that, on his own account, he occasioned me uneasiness. If he would but have named a single relative or friend, I would instantly have written, and urged their taking the poor fellow away to some convenient retreat. But he seemed alone, absolutely alone in the universe. A bit of wreck in the mid-Atlantic. At length, necessities connected with my business tyrannized over all other considerations. Decently as I could, I told Bartleby that in six days' time he must unconditionally leave the office. I warned him to take measures, in the interval, for procuring some other abode. I offered to assist him in this endeavor, if he himself would but take the first step towards a removal. "And when you finally quit me, Bartleby," added I, "I shall see that you go not away entirely unprovided. Six days from this hour, remember."

135 At the expiration of that period, I peeped behind the screen, and lo! Bartleby was there.

136 I buttoned up my coat, balanced myself; advanced slowly towards him, touched his shoulder, and said, "The time has come; you must quit this place; I am sorry for you; here is money; but you must go."

137 "I would prefer not," he replied, with his back still towards me.

138 "You *must*."

NOTES

139 He remained silent.

140 Now I had an unbounded confidence in this man's common honesty. He had frequently restored to me sixpences and shillings carelessly dropped upon the floor, for I am apt to be very reckless in such shirt-button affairs. The proceeding then which followed will not be deemed extraordinary.

141 "Bartleby," said I, "I owe you twelve dollars on account; here are thirty-two; the odd twenty are yours.—Will you take it?" and I handed the bills towards him.

142 But he made no motion.

143 "I will leave them here then," putting them under a weight on the table. Then taking my hat and cane and going to the door I tranquilly turned and added—"After you have removed your things from these offices, Bartleby, you will of course lock the door—since every one is now gone for the day but you—and if you please, slip your key underneath the mat, so that I may have it in the morning. I shall not see you again; so good-bye to you. If hereafter in your new place of abode I can be of any service to you, do not fail to advise me by letter. Good-bye, Bartleby, and fare you well."

144 But he answered not a word; like the last column of some ruined temple, he remained standing mute and solitary in the middle of the otherwise deserted room.

145 As I walked home in a pensive mood, my vanity got the better of my pity. I could not but highly plume myself on my masterly management in getting rid of Bartleby. Masterly I call it, and such it must appear to any dispassionate thinker. The beauty of my procedure seemed to consist in its perfect quietness. There was no vulgar bullying, no bravado of any sort, no choleric hectoring, and striding to and fro across the apartment, jerking out vehement commands for Bartleby to bundle himself off with his beggarly traps. Nothing of the kind. Without loudly bidding Bartleby depart—as an inferior genius might have done—I *assumed* the ground that depart he must; and upon that assumption built all I had to say. The more I thought over my procedure, the more I was charmed with it. Nevertheless, next morning, upon awakening, I had my doubts,—I had somehow slept off the fumes of vanity. One of the coolest and wisest hours a man has, is just after he awakes in the morning. My procedure seemed as sagacious as ever—but only in theory. How it would prove in practice—there was the rub. It was truly a beautiful thought to have assumed Bartleby's departure; but, after all, that assumption was simply my own, and none of Bartleby's. The great point was, not whether I had assumed that he would quit me, but whether he would prefer so to do. He was more a man of preferences than assumptions.

146 After breakfast, I walked down town, arguing the probabilities *pro* and *con*. One moment I thought it would prove a miserable failure, and Bartleby would

NOTES

be found all alive at my office as usual; the next moment it seemed certain that I should see his chair empty. And so I kept veering about. At the corner of Broadway and Canal-street, I saw quite an excited group of people standing in earnest conversation.

147 "I'll take odds he doesn't," said a voice as I passed.

148 "Doesn't go?—done!" said I, "put up your money."

149 I was instinctively putting my hand in my pocket to produce my own, when I remembered that this was an election day. The words I had overheard bore no reference to Bartleby, but to the success or non-success of some candidate for the mayoralty. In my intent frame of mind, I had, as it were, imagined that all Broadway shared in my excitement, and were debating the same question with me. I passed on, very thankful that the uproar of the street screened my momentary absent-mindedness.

150 As I had intended, I was earlier than usual at my office door. I stood listening for a moment. All was still. He must be gone. I tried the knob. The door was locked. Yes, my procedure had worked to a charm; he indeed must be vanished. Yet a certain melancholy mixed with this: I was almost sorry for my brilliant success. I was fumbling under the door mat for the key, which Bartleby was to have left there for me, when accidentally my knee knocked against a panel, producing a summoning sound, and in response a voice came to me from within—"Not yet; I am occupied."

151 It was Bartleby.

152 I was thunderstruck. For an instant I stood like the man who, pipe in mouth, was killed one cloudless afternoon long ago in Virginia, by a summer lightning; at his own warm open window he was killed, and remained leaning out there upon the dreamy afternoon, till some one touched him, when he fell.

153 "Not gone!" I murmured at last. But again obeying that wondrous ascendancy which the inscrutable scrivener had over me, and from which ascendancy, for all my chafing, I could not completely escape, I slowly went down stairs and out into the street, and while walking round the block, considered what I should next do in this unheard-of perplexity. Turn the man out by an actual thrusting I could not; to drive him away by calling him hard names would not do; calling in the police was an unpleasant idea; and yet, permit him to enjoy his cadaverous triumph over me,—this too I could not think of. What was to be done? Or, if nothing could be done, was there any thing further that I could *assume* in the matter? Yes, as before I had prospectively assumed that Bartleby would depart, so now I might retrospectively assume that departed he was. In the legitimate carrying out of this assumption, I might enter my office in a great hurry, and pretending not to see Bartleby at all, walk straight against him as if he were air. Such a proceeding would in a singular degree

NOTES

have the appearance of a home-thrust. It was hardly possible that Bartleby could withstand such an application of the doctrine of assumptions. But upon second thoughts the success of the plan seemed rather dubious. I resolved to argue the matter over with him again.

154 "Bartleby," said I, entering the office, with a quietly severe expression, "I am seriously displeased. I am pained, Bartleby. I had thought better of you. I had imagined you of such a gentlemanly organization, that in any delicate dilemma a slight hint would have suffice—in short, an assumption. But it appears I am deceived. Why," I added, unaffectedly starting, "you have not even touched that money yet," pointing to it, just where I had left it the evening previous.

155 He answered nothing.

156 "Will you, or will you not, quit me?" I now demanded in a sudden passion, advancing close to him.

157 "I would prefer *not* to quit you," he replied, gently emphasizing the *not*.

158 "What earthly right have you to stay here? Do you pay any rent? Do you pay my taxes? Or is this property yours?"

159 He answered nothing.

160 "Are you ready to go on and write now? Are your eyes recovered? Could you copy a small paper for me this morning? or help examine a few lines? or step round to the post-office? In a word, will you do any thing at all, to give a coloring to your refusal to depart the premises?"

161 He silently retired into his hermitage.

162 I was now in such a state of nervous resentment that I thought it but prudent to check myself at present from further demonstrations. Bartleby and I were alone. I remembered the tragedy of the unfortunate Adams and the still more unfortunate Colt in the solitary office of the latter; and how poor Colt, being dreadfully incensed by Adams, and imprudently permitting himself to get wildly excited, was at unawares hurried into his fatal act—an act which certainly no man could possibly deplore more than the actor himself. Often it had occurred to me in my ponderings upon the subject, that had that altercation taken place in the public street, or at a private residence, it would not have terminated as it did. It was the circumstance of being alone in a solitary office, up stairs, of a building entirely unhallowed by humanizing domestic associations—an uncarpeted office, doubtless, of a dusty, haggard sort of appearance;—this it must have been, which greatly helped to enhance the irritable desperation of the hapless Colt.

163 But when this old Adam of resentment rose in me and tempted me concerning Bartleby, I grappled him and threw him. How? Why, simply by recalling the

NOTES

divine injunction: "A new commandment give I unto you, that ye love one another." Yes, this it was that saved me. Aside from higher considerations, charity often operates as a vastly wise and prudent principle—a great safeguard to its possessor. Men have committed murder for jealousy's sake, and anger's sake, and hatred's sake, and selfishness' sake, and spiritual pride's sake; but no man that ever I heard of, ever committed a diabolical murder for sweet charity's sake. Mere self-interest, then, if no better motive can be enlisted, should, especially with high-tempered men, prompt all beings to charity and philanthropy. At any rate, upon the occasion in question, I strove to drown my exasperated feelings towards the scrivener by benevolently construing his conduct. Poor fellow, poor fellow! thought I, he don't mean any thing; and besides, he has seen hard times, and ought to be indulged.

164 I endeavored also immediately to occupy myself, and at the same time to comfort my despondency. I tried to fancy that in the course of the morning, at such time as might prove agreeable to him. Bartleby, of his own free accord, would emerge from his hermitage, and take up some decided line of march in the direction of the door. But no. Half-past twelve o'clock came; Turkey began to glow in the face, overturn his inkstand, and become generally obstreperous; Nippers abated down into quietude and courtesy; Ginger Nut munched his noon apple; and Bartleby remained standing at his window in one of his profoundest dead-wall reveries. Will it be credited? Ought I to acknowledge it? That afternoon I left the office without saying one further word to him.

165 Some days now passed, during which, at leisure intervals I looked a little into "Edwards on the Will," and "Priestley on Necessity." Under the circumstances, those books induced a salutary feeling. Gradually I slid into the persuasion that these troubles of mine touching the scrivener, had been all predestinated from eternity, and Bartleby was billeted upon me for some mysterious purpose of an all-wise Providence, which it was not for a mere mortal like me to fathom. Yes, Bartleby, stay there behind your screen, thought I; I shall persecute you no more; you are harmless and noiseless as any of these old chairs; in short, I never feel so private as when I know you are here. At last I see it, I feel it; I penetrate to the predestinated purpose of my life. I am content. Others may have loftier parts to enact; but my mission in this world, Bartleby, is to furnish you with office-room for such period as you may see fit to remain.

166 I believe that this wise and blessed frame of mind would have continued with me, had it not been for the unsolicited and uncharitable remarks obtruded upon me by my professional friends who visited the rooms. But thus it often is, that the constant friction of illiberal minds wears out at last the best resolves of the more generous. Though to be sure, when I reflected upon it, it was not strange that people entering my office should be struck by the peculiar aspect of the unaccountable Bartleby, and so be tempted to throw out some

NOTES

sinister observations concerning him. Sometimes an attorney having business with me, and calling at my office and finding no one but the scrivener there, would undertake to obtain some sort of precise information from him touching my whereabouts; but without heeding his idle talk, Bartleby would remain standing immovable in the middle of the room. So after contemplating him in that position for a time, the attorney would depart, no wiser than he came.

167 Also, when a Reference was going on, and the room full of lawyers and witnesses and business was driving fast; some deeply occupied legal gentleman present, seeing Bartleby wholly unemployed, would request him to run round to his (the legal gentleman's) office and fetch some papers for him. Thereupon, Bartleby would tranquilly decline, and yet remain idle as before. Then the lawyer would give a great stare, and turn to me. And what could I say? At last I was made aware that all through the circle of my professional acquaintance, a whisper of wonder was running round, having reference to the strange creature I kept at my office. This worried me very much. And as the idea came upon me of his possibly turning out a long-lived man, and keep occupying my chambers, and denying my authority; and perplexing my visitors; and scandalizing my professional reputation; and casting a general gloom over the premises; keeping soul and body together to the last upon his savings (for doubtless he spent but half a dime a day), and in the end perhaps outlive me, and claim possession of my office by right of his perpetual occupancy: as all these dark anticipations crowded upon me more and more, and my friends continually intruded their relentless remarks upon the apparition in my room; a great change was wrought in me. I resolved to gather all my faculties together, and for ever rid me of this intolerable incubus.

168 Ere revolving any complicated project, however, adapted to this end, I first simply suggested to Bartleby the propriety of his permanent departure. In a calm and serious tone, I commended the idea to his careful and mature consideration. But having taken three days to meditate upon it, he apprised me that his original determination remained the same in short, that he still preferred to abide with me.

169 What shall I do? I now said to myself, buttoning up my coat to the last button. What shall I do? what ought I to do? what does conscience say I *should* do with this man, or rather ghost. Rid myself of him, I must; go, he shall. But how? You will not thrust him, the poor, pale, passive mortal,— you will not thrust such a helpless creature out of your door? You will not dishonor yourself by such cruelty? No, I will not, I cannot do that. Rather would I let him live and die here, and then mason up his remains in the wall. What then will you do? For all your coaxing, he will not budge. Bribes he leaves under your own paperweight on your table; in short, it is quite plain that he prefers to cling to you.

NOTES

170 Then something severe, something unusual must be done. What! Surely you will not have him collared by a constable, and commit his innocent pallor to the common jail? And upon what ground could you procure such a thing to be done?—a vagrant, is he? What! He a vagrant, a wanderer, who refuses to budge? It is because he will *not* be a vagrant, then, that you seek to count him *as* a vagrant. That is too absurd. No visible means of support: there I have him. Wrong again: for indubitably he *does* support himself, and that is the only unanswerable proof that any man can show of his possessing the means so to do. No more then. Since he will not quit me, I must quit him. I will change my offices; I will move elsewhere; and give him fair notice, that if I find him on my new premises I will then proceed against him as a common trespasser.

171 Acting accordingly, next day I thus addressed him: "I find these chambers too far from the City Hall; the air is unwholesome. In a word, I propose to remove my offices next week, and shall no longer require your services. I tell you this now, in order that you may seek another place." He made no reply, and nothing more was said.

172 On the appointed day I engaged carts and men, proceeded to my chambers, and having but little furniture, every thing was removed in a few hours. Throughout, the scrivener remained standing behind the screen, which I directed to be removed the last thing. It was withdrawn; and being folded up like a huge folio, left him the motionless occupant of a naked room. I stood in the entry watching him a moment, while something from within me upbraided me.

173 I re-entered, with my hand in my pocket—and—and my heart in my mouth.

174 "Good-bye, Bartleby; I am going—good-bye, and God some way bless you; and take that," slipping something in his hand. But it dropped upon the floor, and then,—strange to say—I tore myself from him whom I had so longed to be rid of.

175 Established in my new quarters, for a day or two I kept the door locked, and started at every footfall in the passages. When I returned to my rooms after any little absence, I would pause at the threshold for an instant, and attentively listen, ere applying my key. But these fears were needless. Bartleby never came nigh me.

176 I thought all was going well, when a perturbed looking stranger visited me, inquiring whether I was the person who had recently occupied rooms at No.—Wall-street.

177 Full of forebodings, I replied that I was.

NOTES

178 "Then sir," said the stranger, who proved a lawyer, "you are responsible for the man you left there. He refuses to do any copying; he refuses to do any thing; he says he prefers not to; and he refuses to quit the premises."

179 "I am very sorry, sir," said I, with assumed tranquillity, but an inward tremor, "but, really, the man you allude to is nothing to me—he is no relation or apprentice of mine, that you should hold me responsible for him."

180 "In mercy's name, who is he?"

181 "I certainly cannot inform you. I know nothing about him. Formerly I employed him as a copyist; but he has done nothing for me now for some time past."

182 "I shall settle him then,—good morning, sir."

183 Several days passed, and I heard nothing more; and though I often felt a charitable prompting to call at the place and see poor Bartleby, yet a certain squeamishness of I know not what withheld me.

184 All is over with him, by this time, thought I at last, when through another week no further intelligence reached me. But coming to my room the day after, I found several persons waiting at my door in a high state of nervous excitement.

185 "That's the man—here he comes," cried the foremost one, whom I recognized as the lawyer who had previously called upon me alone.

186 "You must take him away, sir, at once," cried a portly person among them, advancing upon me, and whom I knew to be the landlord of No.— Wall-street. "These gentlemen, my tenants, cannot stand it any longer; Mr. B—" pointing to the lawyer, "has turned him out of his room, and he now persists in haunting the building generally, sitting upon the banisters of the stairs by day, and sleeping in the entry by night. Every body is concerned; clients are leaving the offices; some fears are entertained of a mob; something you must do, and that without delay."

187 Aghast at this torrent, I fell back before it, and would fain have locked myself in my new quarters. In vain I persisted that Bartleby was nothing to me—no more than to any one else. In vain:—I was the last person known to have any thing to do with him, and they held me to the terrible account. Fearful then of being exposed in the papers (as one person present obscurely threatened) I considered the matter, and at length said, that if the lawyer would give me a confidential interview with the scrivener, in his (the lawyer's) own room, I would that afternoon strive my best to rid them of the nuisance they complained of.

188 Going up stairs to my old haunt, there was Bartleby silently sitting upon the banister at the landing.

189 "What are you doing here, Bartleby?" said I.

NOTES

190 "Sitting upon the banister," he mildly replied.

191 I motioned him into the lawyer's room, who then left us.

192 "Bartleby," said I, "are you aware that you are the cause of great tribulation to me, by persisting in occupying the entry after being dismissed from the office?"

193 No answer.

194 "Now one of two things must take place. Either you must do something, or something must be done to you. Now what sort of business would you like to engage in? Would you like to re-engage in copying for some one?"

195 "No; I would prefer not to make any change."

196 "Would you like a clerkship in a dry-goods store?"

197 "There is too much confinement about that. No, I would not like a clerkship; but I am not particular."

198 "Too much confinement," I cried, "why you keep yourself confined all the time!"

199 "I would prefer not to take a clerkship," he rejoined, as if to settle that little item at once.

200 "How would a bar-tender's business suit you? There is no trying of the eyesight in that."

201 "I would not like it at all; though, as I said before, I am not particular."

202 His unwonted wordiness inspirited me. I returned to the charge.

203 "Well then, would you like to travel through the country collecting bills for the merchants? That would improve your health."

204 "No, I would prefer to be doing something else."

205 "How then would going as a companion to Europe, to entertain some young gentleman with your conversation,—how would that suit you?"

206 "Not at all. It does not strike me that there is any thing definite about that. I like to be stationary. But I am not particular."

207 "Stationary you shall be then," I cried, now losing all patience, and for the first time in all my exasperating connection with him fairly flying into a passion. "If you do not go away from these premises before night, I shall feel bound—indeed I *am* bound—to—to—to quit the premises myself!" I rather absurdly concluded, knowing not with what possible threat to try to frighten his immobility into compliance. Despairing of all further efforts, I was precipitately

NOTES

leaving him, when a final thought occurred to me—one which had not been wholly unindulged before.

208 "Bartleby," said I, in the kindest tone I could assume under such exciting circumstances, "will you go home with me now—not to my office, but my dwelling—and remain there till we can conclude upon some convenient arrangement for you at our leisure? Come, let us start now, right away."

209 "No: at present I would prefer not to make any change at all."

210 I answered nothing; but effectually dodging every one by the suddenness and rapidity of my flight, rushed from the building, ran up Wall-street towards Broadway, and jumping into the first omnibus was soon removed from pursuit. As soon as tranquillity returned I distinctly perceived that I had now done all that I possibly could, both in respect to the demands of the landlord and his tenants, and with regard to my own desire and sense of duty, to benefit Bartleby, and shield him from rude persecution. I now strove to be entirely care-free and quiescent; and my conscience justified me in the attempt; though indeed it was not so successful as I could have wished. So fearful was I of being again hunted out by the incensed landlord and his exasperated tenants, that, surrendering my business to Nippers, for a few days I drove about the upper part of the town and through the suburbs, in my rockaway; crossed over to Jersey City and Hoboken, and paid fugitive visits to Manhattanville and Astoria. In fact I almost lived in my rockaway for the time.

211 When again I entered my office, lo, a note from the landlord lay upon the desk. I opened it with trembling hands. It informed me that the writer had sent to the police, and had Bartleby removed to the Tombs as a vagrant. Moreover, since I knew more about him than any one else, he wished me to appear at that place, and make a suitable statement of the facts. These tidings had a conflicting effect upon me. At first I was indignant; but at last almost approved. The landlord's energetic, summary disposition had led him to adopt a procedure which I do not think I would have decided upon myself; and yet as a last resort, under such peculiar circumstances, it seemed the only plan.

212 As I afterwards learned, the poor scrivener, when told that he must be conducted to the Tombs, offered not the slightest obstacle, but in his pale unmoving way, silently acquiesced.

213 Some of the compassionate and curious bystanders joined the party; and headed by one of the constables arm in arm with Bartleby, the silent procession filed its way through all the noise, and heat, and joy of the roaring thoroughfares at noon.

214 The same day I received the note I went to the Tombs, or to speak more properly, the Halls of Justice. Seeking the right officer, I stated the purpose of my call, and was informed that the individual I described was indeed within. I

NOTES

then assured the functionary that Bartleby was a perfectly honest man, and greatly to be compassionated, however unaccountably eccentric. I narrated all I knew, and closed by suggesting the idea of letting him remain in as indulgent confinement as possible till something less harsh might be done—though indeed I hardly knew what. At all events, if nothing else could be decided upon, the alms-house must receive him. I then begged to have an interview.

215 Being under no disgraceful charge, and quite serene and harmless in all his ways, they had permitted him freely to wander about the prison, and especially in the inclosed grass-platted yard thereof. And so I found him there, standing all alone in the quietest of the yards, his face towards a high wall, while all around, from the narrow slits of the jail windows, I thought I saw peering out upon him the eyes of murderers and thieves.

216 "Bartleby!"

217 "I know you," he said, without looking round,—"and I want nothing to say to you."

218 "It was not I that brought you here, Bartleby," said I, keenly pained at his implied suspicion. "And to you, this should not be so vile a place. Nothing reproachful attaches to you by being here. And see, it is not so sad a place as one might think. Look, there is the sky, and here is the grass."

219 "I know where I am," he replied, but would say nothing more, and so I left him.

220 As I entered the corridor again, a broad meat-like man, in an apron, accosted me, and jerking his thumb over his shoulder said—"Is that your friend?"

221 "Yes."

222 "Does he want to starve? If he does, let him live on the prison fare, that's all."

223 "Who are you?" asked I, not knowing what to make of such an unofficially speaking person in such a place.

224 "I am the grub-man. Such gentlemen as have friends here, hire me to provide them with something good to eat."

225 "Is this so?" said I, turning to the turnkey.

226 He said it was.

227 "Well then," said I, slipping some silver into the grub-man's hands (for so they called him). "I want you to give particular attention to my friend there; let him have the best dinner you can get. And you must be as polite to him as possible."

NOTES

228 "Introduce me, will you?" said the grub-man, looking at me with an expression which seem to say he was all impatience for an opportunity to give a specimen of his breeding.

229 Thinking it would prove of benefit to the scrivener, I acquiesced; and asking the grub-man his name, went up with him to Bartleby.

230 "Bartleby, this is Mr. Cutlets; you will find him very useful to you."

231 "Your servant, sir, your servant," said the grub-man, making a low salutation behind his apron. "Hope you find it pleasant here, sir;—spacious grounds—cool apartments, sir—hope you'll stay with us some time—try to make it agreeable. May Mrs. Cutlets and I have the pleasure of your company to dinner, sir, in Mrs. Cutlets' private room?"

232 "I prefer not to dine to-day," said Bartleby, turning away. "It would disagree with me; I am unused to dinners." So saying he slowly moved to the other side of the enclosure, and took up a position fronting the dead-wall.

233 "How's this?" said the grub-man, addressing me with a stare of astonishment. "He's odd, ain't he?"

234 "I think he is a little deranged," said I, sadly.

235 "Deranged? deranged is it? Well now, upon my word, I thought that friend of yourn was a gentleman forger; they are always pale and genteel-like, them forgers. I can't pity 'em—can't help it, sir. Did you know Monroe Edwards?" he added touchingly, and paused. Then, laying his hand pityingly on my shoulder, sighed, "He died of consumption at Sing-Sing. So you weren't acquainted with Monroe?"

236 "No, I was never socially acquainted with any forgers. But I cannot stop longer. Look to my friend yonder. You will not lose by it. I will see you again."

237 Some few days after this, I again obtained admission to the Tombs, and went through the corridors in quest of Bartleby; but without finding him.

238 "I saw him coming from his cell not long ago," said a turnkey, "may be he's gone to loiter in the yards."

239 So I went in that direction. "Are you looking for the silent man?" said another turnkey passing me. "Yonder he lies—sleeping in the yard there. 'Tis not twenty minutes since I saw him lie down."

240 The yard was entirely quiet. It was not accessible to the common prisoners. The surrounding walls, of amazing thickness, kept off all sounds behind them. The Egyptian character of the masonry weighed upon me with its gloom. But a soft imprisoned turf grew under foot. The heart of the eternal pyramids, it seemed, wherein, by some strange magic, through the clefts, grass-seed, dropped by birds, had sprung.

NOTES

241 Strangely huddled at the base of the wall, his knees drawn up, and lying on his side, his head touching the cold stones, I saw the wasted Bartleby. But nothing stirred. I paused; then went close up to him; stooped over, and saw that his dim eyes were open; otherwise he seemed profoundly sleeping. Something prompted me to touch him. I felt his hand, when a tingling shiver ran up my arm and down my spine to my feet.

242 The round face of the grub-man peered upon me now. "His dinner is ready. Won't he dine to-day, either? Or does he live without dining?"

243 "Lives without dining," said I, and closed his eyes.

244 "Eh!—He's asleep, ain't he?"

245 "With kings and counselors," murmured I.

• • •

246 There would seem little need for proceeding further in this history. Imagination will readily supply the meager recital of poor Bartleby's interment. But ere parting with the reader, let me say, that if this little narrative has sufficiently interested him, to awaken curiosity as to who Bartleby was, and what manner of life he led prior to the present narrator's making his acquaintance, I can only reply, that in such curiosity I fully share, but am wholly unable to gratify it. Yet here I hardly know whether I should divulge one little item of rumor, which came to my ear a few months after the scrivener's decease. Upon what basis it rested, I could never ascertain; and hence, how true it is I cannot now tell. But inasmuch as this vague report has not been without certain strange suggestive interest to me, however sad, it may prove the same with some others; and so I will briefly mention it. The report was this: that Bartleby had been a subordinate clerk in the Dead Letter Office at Washington, from which he had been suddenly removed by a change in the administration. When I think over this rumor, I cannot adequately express the emotions which seize me. Dead letters! does it not sound like dead men? Conceive a man by nature and misfortune prone to a pallid hopelessness, can any business seem more fitted to heighten it than that of continually handling these dead letters, and assorting them for the flames? For by the cart-load they are annually burned. Sometimes from out the folded paper the pale clerk takes a ring:—the finger it was meant for, perhaps, moulders in the grave; a bank-note sent in swiftest charity:—he whom it would relieve, nor eats nor hungers any more; pardon for those who died despairing; hope for those who died unhoping; good tidings for those who died stifled by unrelieved calamities. On errands of life, these letters speed to death.

247 Ah Bartleby! Ah humanity!

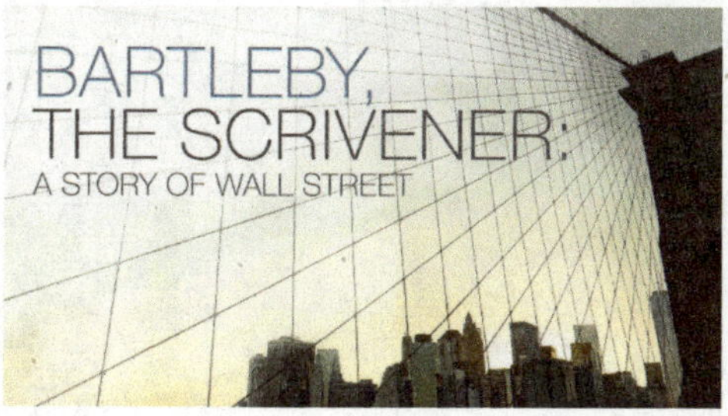

First Read

Read "Bartleby, the Scrivener: A Story of Wall Street." After you read, complete the Think Questions below.

THINK QUESTIONS

1. How does the narrator meet Bartleby? Cite specific evidence from the text to support your answer.

2. How does Turkey respond to Bartleby's refusal to have his work examined by the other scriveners? Cite evidence from the text in support of your answer.

3. What is one idea of Bartleby that the narrator has to rid himself of after the scrivener refuses to leave? Use evidence from the text to support your answer.

4. Use context clues to determine the meaning of the word **alacrity** as it is used in the text. Write your definition of *alacrity* here, and explain which clues helped you figure it out.

5. Keeping in mind that the Latin word *prūdēns* means "wise," determine the meaning of the word **prudent** as it is used in the text. Write your definition of *prudent* here, and explain how you figured it out.

Skill: Theme

Use the Checklist to analyze Theme in "Bartleby, the Scrivener: A Story of Wall Street." Refer to the sample student annotations about Theme in the text.

••• CHECKLIST FOR THEME

In order to identify two or more themes of a text, note the following:

- ✓ the subject and how it relates to the themes in the text
- ✓ if one or more themes are stated directly in the text
- ✓ details in the text that help to reveal each theme:
  - the title and chapter headings
  - details about the setting
  - the narrator's or speaker's tone
  - characters' thoughts, actions, and dialogue
  - the central conflict, climax, and resolution of the conflict
  - shifts in characters, setting, or plot events
- ✓ when the themes interact with each other

To determine two or more themes of a text and analyze their development over the course of the text, including how they interact and build on one another to produce a complex account, consider the following questions:

- ✓ What are the themes in the text? When do they emerge?
- ✓ How does each theme develop over the course of the text?
- ✓ How do the themes interact and build on one another?

Skill: Theme

Reread paragraphs 95–108 from “Bartleby, the Scrivener: A Story of Wall Street.” Then, using the Checklist on the previous page, answer the multiple-choice questions below.

YOUR TURN

1. How does the dialogue between the narrator and Bartleby further develop the theme related to loneliness and isolation?

   - A. It shows that Bartleby’s growing friendship with the narrator proves that even lonely people can make friends if they want to.
   - B. It reveals that the narrator accepts Bartleby’s dangerous behavior, which may help Bartleby overcome his isolation.
   - C. It describes Bartleby as a person who thinks more of himself than others and how this attitude causes his relationships to fail.
   - D. It indicates Bartleby’s entrenchment in his isolation and how his pride and refusal to talk only further separate him from people.

2. What impact does Bartleby’s nonconformity to social norms have on the narrator’s view of him?

   - A. He believes Bartleby’s poor eyesight is responsible and offers to help him with medical expenses.
   - B. He is persuaded that Bartleby is violent and calls the police to take him to the Tombs.
   - C. He thinks Bartleby is ungrateful for his help, which increases the barrier between them.
   - D. He begins to see Bartleby as a free spirit and wishes to spend more time with him.

Skill: Point of View

Use the Checklist to analyze Point of View in "Bartleby, the Scrivener: A Story of Wall Street." Refer to the sample student annotations about Point of View in the text.

••• CHECKLIST FOR POINT OF VIEW

In order to determine a narrator's point of view through what is directly stated is different from what is really meant, note the following:

- ✓ literary techniques intended to provide humor or criticism. Examples include:
  - sarcasm, or the use of language that says one thing but means the opposite
  - irony, or a contrast between what one expects to happen and what happens
  - understatement, or an instance where a character deliberately makes a situation seem less important or serious than it is
  - satire, or the use of humor, irony, exaggeration, or ridicule to expose and criticize people's foolishness or vices
- ✓ possible critiques an author might be making about contemporary society
- ✓ an unreliable narrator or character whose point of view cannot be trusted

To analyze a case in which grasping a point of view requires distinguishing what is directly stated in a text from what is really meant, consider the following questions:

- ✓ How do the cultural lens and experiences of the narrator or speaker shape point of view? How do cultural lens and experiences shape what they say and how they say it?
- ✓ Is the narrator or speaker reliable? Why?
- ✓ How does a character's or narrator's point of view contribute to a non-literal understanding of the text?
- ✓ How does the use of sarcasm, understatement, or satire add meaning to the story?

Skill: Point of View

Reread paragraphs 12 and 13 from "Bartleby, the Scrivener: A Story of Wall Street." Then, using the Checklist on the previous page, answer the multiple-choice questions below.

YOUR TURN

1. This question has two parts. First, answer Part A. Then, answer Part B.

Part A: What is the main aspect of office culture being satirized in this excerpt?

- ○ A. lack of productivity
- ○ B. substandard office equipment
- ○ C. difficulties with the boss's temper
- ○ D. individualism in the workplace

Part B: Which line from the excerpt best supports the satirical message in Part A?

- ○ A. "I was well persuaded that whatever might be his faults in other respects, he was, at least, a temperate young man"
- ○ B. "nature herself seemed to have been his vintner, and at his birth charged him so thoroughly with an irritable, brandy-like disposition"
- ○ C. "I plainly perceive that for Nippers, brandy and water were altogether superfluous."
- ○ D. "When Nippers' was on, Turkey's was off; and *vice versa*."

2. Which line from the excerpt supports this satirical message by explanation: "Their fits relieved each other like guards"?

- ○ A. "for Nippers, brandy and water were altogether superfluous"
- ○ B. "When Nippers' was on, Turkey's was off; and vice versa."
- ○ C. "This was a good natural arrangement under the circumstances."
- ○ D. "I never had to do with their eccentricities at one time."

Skill: Figurative Language

Use the Checklist to analyze Figurative Language in “Bartleby, the Scrivener: A Story of Wall Street.” Refer to the sample student annotations about Figurative Language in the text.

••• CHECKLIST FOR FIGURATIVE LANGUAGE

In order to determine the meaning of a figure of speech in context, note the following:

- ✓ words and phrases that mean one thing literally and suggest something else
- ✓ similes, metaphors, or personification
- ✓ figures of speech, including
    - paradoxes, or a seemingly contradictory statement that when further investigated or explained proves to be true, such as
        - a character described as “a wise fool”
        - a character stating, “I must be cruel to be kind”
    - hyperbole, or exaggerated statements not meant to be taken literally, such as
        - a child saying, “I’ll be doing this homework until I’m 100!”
        - a claim such as “I’m so hungry I could eat a horse!”

In order to interpret a figure of speech in context and analyze its role in the text, consider the following questions:

- ✓ Where is there figurative language in the text, and what seems to be the author’s purpose in using it?
- ✓ Why does the author use a figure of speech rather than literal language?
- ✓ What impact does exaggeration or hyperbole have on your understanding of the text?
- ✓ Where are there examples of paradoxes, and how do they affect the meaning in the text?
- ✓ Where are contradictory words and phrases used to enhance the reader’s understanding of the character, object, or idea?
- ✓ How does the figurative language develop the message or themes of the literary work?

Skill: Figurative Language

Reread paragraph 53 from "Bartleby, the Scrivener: A Story of Wall Street." Then, using the Checklist on the previous page, answer the multiple-choice questions below.

YOUR TURN

1. Which of the following sentences from the paragraph contains an an example of paradox?

   - O A. Nothing so aggravates an earnest person as a passive resistance.
   - O B. Even so, for the most part, I regarded Bartleby and his ways.
   - O C. If I turn him away, the chances are he will fall in with some less indulgent employer, and then he will be rudely treated, and perhaps driven forth miserably to starve.
   - O D. The passiveness of Bartleby sometimes irritated me.

2. How does the use of paradox from Question 1 serve to enhance the reader's understanding of Bartleby's character?

   - O A. It demonstrates the strong relationship between the narrator and Bartleby.
   - O B. It helps the reader to see him in a more favorable light.
   - O C. It highlights his strangeness and the narrator's confusion towards him.
   - O D. It helps the reader to see what motivates his actions as a character.

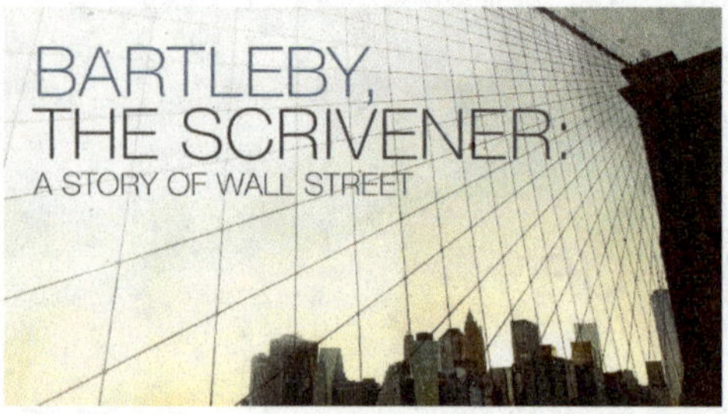

Close Read

Reread "Bartleby, the Scrivener: A Story of Wall Street." As you reread, complete the Skills Focus questions below. Then use your answers and annotations from the questions to help you complete the Write activity.

SKILLS FOCUS

1. Satire is a literary technique for criticizing people's foolishness or vices through humor, to inspire improvement. Find an example of satire in the story and explain its impact on the reader.

2. Identify details from paragraph 17 that help readers visualize the arrangement of the law office. Explain how theme emerges in the arrangement of rooms and desks.

3. The author uses figurative language throughout the story. Find an example and explain the effect of your example on the reader.

4. Determine how the narrator's information about Bartleby's past in paragraph 246 helps develop the themes in this story.

5. How do different characters react to Bartleby when his behavior breaks away from expected office behavior? Identify evidence from the text to support your answer. What do these reactions suggest about how humans respond to those who don't fit the norm?

WRITE

LITERARY ANALYSIS: How does Melville use a satirical point of view as well as figurative language to develop the themes in the story? Identify at least one satirical critique in the story and one use of figurative language, and explain how these literary devices help develop the story's themes. Use evidence from the text to support your response.

LITERARY SEMINAR:

Speaking for Social Change

INFORMATIONAL TEXT
StudySync
2018

Introduction

Before the dawn of radio, television, or the internet, social crusaders spoke to crowds. Rousing speeches drew popular attention in the early half of the nineteenth century, especially during the Age of Reform. Delivering great oratory that drew on a mixture of high eloquence and force, activists like Sojourner Truth and Frederick Douglass fought for various causes. Speeches against sexism, slavery, or even the excessive consumption of alcohol were valuable tools for uniting people and movements.

“Good speakers were the celebrities of their day.”

NOTES

1 As the United States moved into the nineteenth century, industrialization and improved technology led to a more robust economy. As a result, the middle class grew and increasingly lived in cities rather than the country. There was now a **critical mass** of people who had the time to engage in social change. To bring these people together and educate them on the important issues of the day, politicians, ministers, and reformers turned to public speaking.

2 As a learned art, public speaking functioned as a status symbol for the middle class. Children were taught oratorical rules and practices in schools, and speeches were used in the home and community. The public could engage either through debate with one another or at lyceums, which were community spaces hosted by local associations that provided public forums for adult education and entertainment. It was not uncommon for lecturers to travel the “lyceum circuit,” going from one town to the next to speak.

3 Good speakers were the celebrities of their day. Eager to be educated, **diverse** audiences, sometimes in the hundreds or thousands, would come to hear a traveling lecturer. People attended local speaking events as a primary method of connecting with their community and reinforcing and debating local beliefs. Larger-than-life orators aimed to capture the minds and hearts of their audience with engaging language and stories from personal experience.

Public Speaking in the Age of Reform

4 In the 1820s, idealistic Americans took part in an outburst of reform movements. They were often inspired by the Second Great Awakening, a major religious movement that reached its peak in the 1820s and 1830s. The Second Great Awakening featured emotional and enthusiastic revival meetings with **dynamic** speakers, which expanded membership and leveraged reform movements to work towards a more perfect society.

5 Whether their motivations were religious or secular, reformers set out to enthrall and influence their audiences in dozens of associations, such as those to end slavery, stop drunkenness, and secure women’s rights.

NOTES

Associations with overlapping and discordant beliefs saw the opportunity to put their beliefs about the social good on the public agenda through public meetings and debates, conventions, and speaking tours.

Temperance

6 For the temperance movement, public speaking was a significant route for spreading awareness. The movement was led by Evangelicals inspired by the Great Awakening, who sought to encourage moderate drinking and, later, complete abstinence from alcohol and changes in laws. Women contributed significantly to these efforts, in part motivated by an attempt to improve women's quality of life, as drunkenness created danger and unpredictability in the home. In fact, women were so important to this effort that the Women's Christian Temperance Union trained women in the skill of public speaking, specifically to spread the message of temperance. Frances Willard, the WCTU's most famous president and a suffragist, would often go on speaking tours, giving 400 lectures a year.

7 Ultimately, efforts by temperance reformers were successful in contributing to a significant decline in the consumption of alcohol. Alcohol prohibition laws were passed by many states beginning in the 1830s.

Anti-Slavery Associations and the Case for Abolition

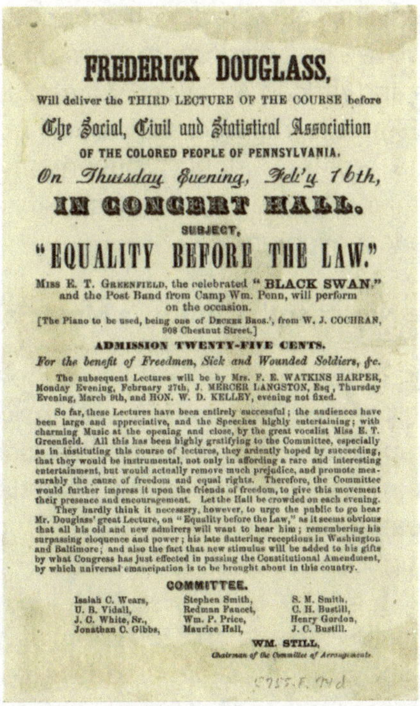

An advertisement for a lecture given by Frederick Douglass in 1865.

NOTES

8 Many religion-based groups also took up the mantle of abolition during and following the Second Great Awakening. Some anti-slavery associations, among these the American Anti-Slavery Society, founded by William Lloyd Garrison, called for the immediate emancipation of enslaved peoples through conventions and meetings. The organization became controversial for its beliefs, leading not only to widespread public outcry but also to protests at some of the speaking events of its members. Frederick Douglass in particular was greatly influenced by William Lloyd Garrison's speaking and joined the American Anti-Slavery Society to tour the Northern states and speak for the cause of abolition.

Women's Suffrage

9 Activism for temperance and the anti-slavery movement helped lay the groundwork for the women's suffrage movement, as women created networks and gained experience as social activists. The women's rights movement is generally described as starting in 1848, with the Seneca Falls Convention. The convention was organized by Lucy Stanton and local female Quakers, including Lucretia Mott, who met Stanton when she was barred from participating at the 1840 World Anti-Slavery Convention in London. Following the Seneca Falls Convention, yearly events including speeches and debates on women's rights and suffrage were organized, and the issue gained traction.

10 Over time, rhetoric shifted to argue that women would bring a moral influence to politics—an argument that garnered more support for women's suffrage than ever before. However, the women's movement was not inclusive of all women; working-class and African American women's issues were not at the forefront of women's suffrage rhetoric. Sojourner Truth's famous "Ain't I a Woman?" speech at a women's rights convention in 1851 critiques the movement for condemning the injustices of slavery while **simultaneously** excluding African American women.

Abraham Lincoln: The Nineteenth Century's Most Famous Orator

11 Public speaking and oratory were an important venue for the marketplace of ideas in the nineteenth century. Politicians' speeches were often the public's only access to the perspectives of their elected officials, and speech carried a great deal of weight in the public's view. Abraham Lincoln is renowned as one of the greatest speakers in American history. His words spoke to a deeply divided audience throughout the Civil War period.

12 In Lincoln's inaugural address, after his election as president in 1860, he pleaded for the North and South to avoid bloodshed and violence. Although the speech is highly regarded today, his plea was not heeded, and on April 12, 1861, Confederate troops attacked Fort Sumter in the harbor of Charleston, South Carolina. The Civil War had begun.

NOTES

Abraham Lincoln's first inaugural address, delivered in front of the U. S. Capitol

13 Two years later, as the Civil War continued, another of Lincoln's famous speeches, his Gettysburg **Address**, helped to dedicate a National Cemetery on the site of the Battle of Gettysburg. In fewer than 300 words, Lincoln describes his vision for the nation and claims that the war was a test to see if a nation striving for equality and self-government could flourish. Many reflect on it now as a testament to the ideals on which the nation was founded and the importance of living those principles. Its opening phrase, "Four score and seven years ago," is among the most recognizable words from any presidential speech.

14 At the time, presidents did not give nearly as many public speeches as they do today. Lincoln was a great orator but differed greatly from other speakers, who could be long-winded, speaking for hours at a time. Lincoln understood the importance that his words would carry, especially because of his earlier political successes due to public speaking. He avoided impromptu opportunities to speak as president, preferring to prepare his remarks.

Nineteenth-Century Speaking Considered in the Present Day

15 The tactics employed in the nineteenth century's most effective speeches can still be seen in some of America's most influential voices today. However, speaking tours are now mostly a thing of the past as technology allows new ways to communicate with millions of people across the world in a variety of forums. From live-streaming videos to social media, individuals are able to share ideas in an instant. However, some argue that reporting of news and writing about ideas necessarily create more distance between speaker and audience and lack the level of participation that these nineteenth-century speaking tours were able to evoke. The powerful oratory of the period engaged citizens and provided a platform for some of the most significant social and political movements of the day, ultimately leading to lasting change, which shaped America's history.

Literary Seminar: Speaking for Social Change

Read "Literary Seminar: Speaking for Social Change." After you read, complete the Think Questions below.

THINK QUESTIONS

1. Why were more people interested in public speaking and social change in the nineteenth century? Explain briefly, using evidence from the text.

2. How did the temperance movement influence public life in the 1830s? Cite evidence from the text to support your response.

3. How is Abraham Lincoln described as a speaker? What were some of his notable speeches?

4. Read the following dictionary entry:

   dynamic
   dy•nam•ic \dī năm' ik\

   noun

   1. a force within a system or process
   2. a level of volume or sound

   adjective

   1. always changing or in motion
   2. full of energy or new ideas

   Which definition most closely matches the meaning of **dynamic** in paragraph 4? Write the correct definition of *dynamic* here and explain how you figured out its meaning.

5. What is the meaning of the word **simultaneously** as it is used in the text? What part of speech is it? Write your best definition of *simultaneously* and explain how you figured it out. Check your answer with a dictionary.

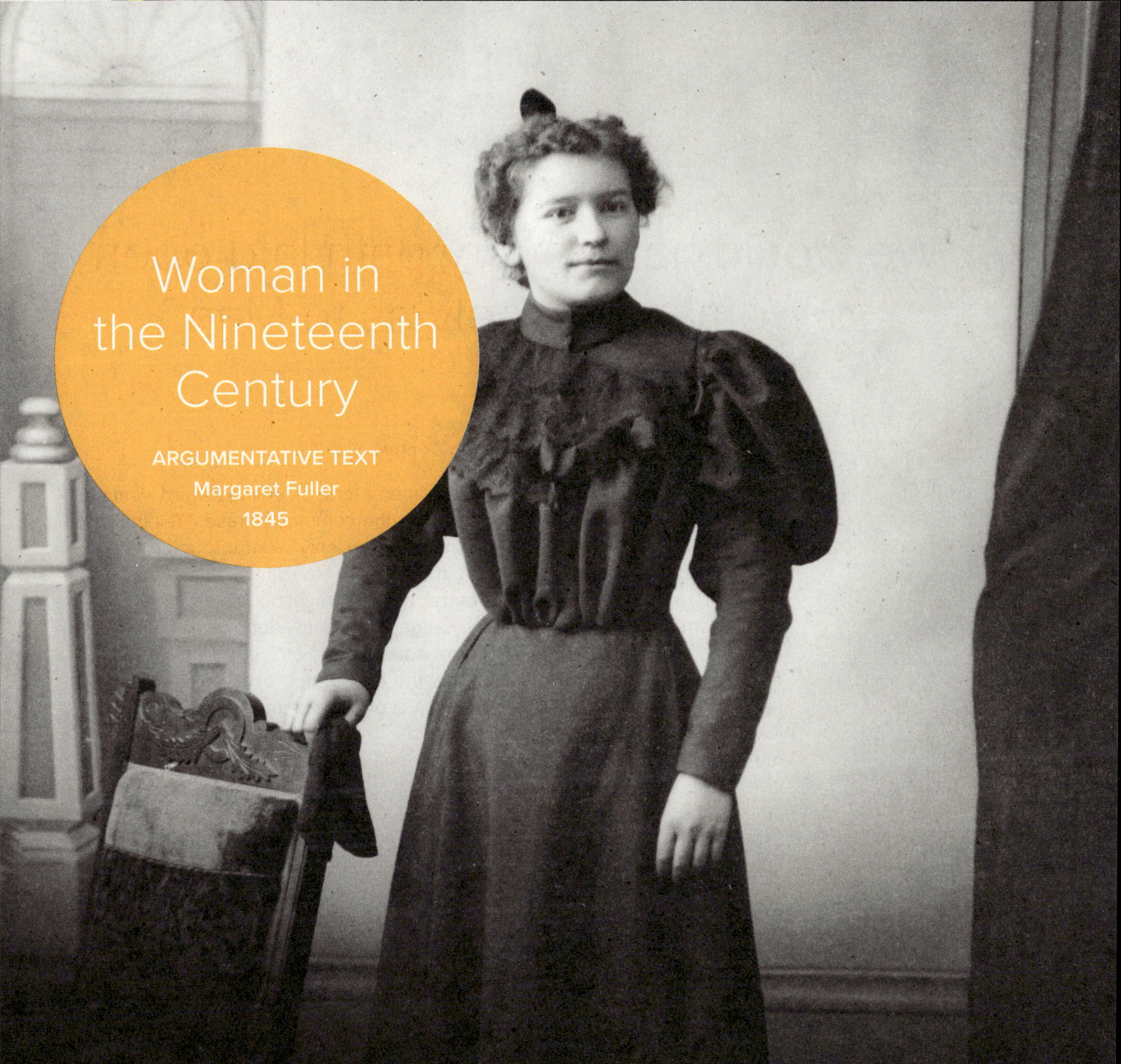

Woman in the Nineteenth Century

ARGUMENTATIVE TEXT
Margaret Fuller
1845

Introduction

Margaret Fuller (1810–1850) was one of the earliest and most vocal supporters of women's rights in the United States. Fuller's book *Woman in the Nineteenth Century* laid the groundwork for the women's suffrage movement, which eventually resulted in the Nineteenth Amendment and women's right to vote. In the excerpt, Fuller focuses on women's social status and concludes that women's issues cannot be advanced unless women are allowed to represent themselves publicly.

"We would have every path laid open to Woman as freely as to Man."

NOTES

from Part I: Woman in the Nineteenth Century

1 Knowing that there exists in the minds of men a tone of feeling toward women as toward slaves, such as is expressed in the common phrase, "Tell that to women and children;" that the infinite soul can only work through them in already ascertained limits; that the gift of reason, Man's highest prerogative, is allotted to them in much lower degree; that they must be kept from mischief and melancholy by being constantly engaged in active labor, which is to be furnished and directed by those better able to think, etc., etc.,—we need not multiply instances, for who can review the experience of last week without recalling words which imply, whether in jest or earnest, these views, or views like these,—knowing this, can we wonder that many reformers think that measures are not likely to be taken in behalf of women, unless their wishes could be publicly represented by women?

2 "That can never be necessary," cry the other side. "All men are privately influenced by women; each has his wife, sister, or female friends, and is too much biased by these relations to fail of representing their interests; and, if this is not enough, let them propose and enforce their wishes with the pen. The beauty of home would be destroyed, the **delicacy** of the sex be violated, the dignity of halls of legislation degraded, by an attempt to introduce them there. Such duties are inconsistent with those of a mother;" and then we have ludicrous pictures of ladies in hysterics at the polls, and senate-chambers filled with cradles.

3 But if, in reply, we admit as truth that Woman seems destined by nature rather for the inner circle, we must add that the arrangements of civilized life have not been, as yet, such as to secure it to her. Her circle, if the duller, is not the quieter. If kept from "excitement," she is not from drudgery. Not only the Indian squaw[1] carries the burdens of the camp, but the favorites of Louis XIV[2]accompany him in his journeys, and the washerwoman stands at her tub, and carries home her work at all seasons, and in all states of health. Those

1. **Indian squaw** an offensive, derogatory term for a North American indigenous woman
2. **Louis XIV** the king of France from 1643 to 1715, known for his gaudy taste and many palaces

NOTES

who think the physical circumstances of Woman would make a part in the affairs of national government unsuitable, are by no means those who think it impossible for negresses to endure field-work, even during pregnancy, or for seamstresses to go through their killing labors.

4 As to the use of the pen, there was quite as much opposition to Woman's possessing herself of that help to free agency as there is now to her seizing on the rostrum or the desk; and she is likely to draw, from a permission to plead her cause that way, opposite inferences to what might be wished by those who now grant it.

5 As to the possibility of her filling with grace and dignity any such position, we should think those who had seen the great actresses, and heard the Quaker[3] preachers of modern times, would not doubt that Woman can express publicly the fulness of thought and creation, without losing any of the peculiar beauty of her sex. What can pollute and tarnish is to act thus from any motive except that something needs to be said or done. Woman could take part in

Women's Suffrage Cartoons, Published in the Late 19th or Early 20th Century, Depicting Different Roles for Women in Society. Rare Book and Special Collections Division, Library of Congress, rbcmil scrp5015401

3. **Quaker** a member of the Religious Society of Friends, a Christian movement devoted to peaceful principles

NOTES

the processions, the songs, the dances of old religion; no one fancied her delicacy was **impaired** by appearing in public for such a cause.

6 As to her home, she is not likely to leave it more than she now does for balls, theatres, meetings for promoting missions, revival meetings, and others to which she flies, in hope of an animation for her existence commensurate with what she sees enjoyed by men. Governors of ladies'-fairs are no less engrossed by such a charge, than the governor of a state by his; presidents of Washingtonian societies no less away from home than presidents of conventions. If men look straitly to it, they will find that, unless their lives are domestic, those of the women will not be. A house is no home unless it contain food and fire for the mind as well as for the body. The female Greek, of our day, is as much in the street as the male to cry, "What news?" We doubt not it was the same in Athens of old. The women, shut out from the market-place, made up for it at the religious festivals. For human beings are not so constituted that they can live without expansion. If they do not get it in one way, they must in another, or perish.

7 As to men's representing women fairly at present, while we hear from men who owe to their wives not only all that is comfortable or graceful, but all that is wise, in the arrangement of their lives, the frequent remark, "You cannot reason with a woman,"—when from those of delicacy, nobleness, and poetic culture, falls the contemptuous phrase "women and children," and that in no light sally of the hour, but in works intended to give a permanent statement of the best experiences,—when not one man, in the million, shall I say? no, not in the hundred million, can rise above the belief that Woman was made for *Man*,—when such traits as these are daily forced upon the attention, can we feel that Man will always do justice to the interests of Woman? Can we think that he takes a sufficiently discerning and religious view of her office and destiny ever to do her justice, except when prompted by sentiment,—accidentally or transiently, that is, for the sentiment will vary according to the relations in which he is placed? The lover, the poet, the artist, are likely to view her nobly. The father and the philosopher have some chance of liberality; the man of the world, the legislator for expediency, none.

8 Under these circumstances, without attaching importance, in themselves, to the changes demanded by the champions of Woman, we hail them as signs of the times. We would have every arbitrary barrier thrown down. We would have every path laid open to Woman as freely as to Man. Were this done, and a slight **temporary** fermentation allowed to subside, we should see crystallizations more pure and of more various beauty. We believe the divine energy would pervade nature to a degree unknown in the history of former ages, and that no discordant collision, but a ravishing harmony of the spheres, would ensue.

NOTES

9 Yet, then and only then will mankind be ripe for this, when inward and outward freedom for Woman as much as for Man shall be acknowledged as a *right*, not yielded as a concession. As the friend of the negro assumes that one man cannot by right hold another in bondage, so should the friend of Woman assume that Man cannot by right lay even well-meant restrictions on Woman. If the negro be a soul, if the woman be a soul, apparelled in flesh, to one Master only are they accountable. There is but one law for souls, and, if there is to be an interpreter of it, he must come not as man, or son of man, but as son of God.

10 Were thought and feeling once so far elevated that Man should esteem himself the brother and friend, but nowise the lord and tutor, of Woman,—were he really bound with her in equal worship,—arrangements as to function and employment would be of no consequence. What Woman needs is not as a woman to act or rule, but as a nature to grow, as an intellect to discern, as a soul to live freely and unimpeded, to unfold such powers as were given her when we left our common home. If fewer talents were given her, yet if allowed the free and full employment of these, so that she may **render** back to the giver his own with usury, she will not complain; nay, I dare to say she will bless and rejoice in her earthly birth-place, her earthly lot. Let us consider what obstructions impede this good era, and what signs give reason to hope that it draws near.

11 I was talking on this subject with Miranda, a woman, who, if any in the world could, might speak without heat and bitterness of the position of her sex. Her father was a man who cherished no sentimental reverence for Woman, but a firm belief in the equality of the sexes. She was his eldest child, and came to him at an age when he needed a companion. From the time she could speak and go alone, he addressed her not as a plaything, but as a living mind. Among the few verses he ever wrote was a copy addressed to this child, when the first locks were cut from her head; and the reverence expressed on this occasion for that cherished head, he never belied. It was to him the temple of immortal intellect. He respected his child, however, too much to be an indulgent parent. He called on her for clear judgment, for courage, for honor and fidelity; in short, for such virtues as he knew. In so far as he possessed the keys to the wonders of this universe, he allowed free use of them to her, and, by the **incentive** of a high expectation, he forbade, so far as possible, that she should let the privilege lie idle.

12 Thus this child was early led to feel herself a child of the spirit. She took her place easily, not only in the world of organized being, but in the world of mind. A dignified sense of self-dependence was given as all her portion, and she found it a sure anchor. Herself securely anchored, her relations with others were established with equal security. She was fortunate in a total absence of those charms which might have drawn to her bewildering

NOTES

flatteries, and in a strong electric nature, which repelled those who did not belong to her, and attracted those who did. With men and women her relations were noble,—affectionate without passion, intellectual without coldness. The world was free to her, and she lived freely in it. Outward adversity came, and inward conflict; but that faith and self-respect had early been awakened which must always lead, at last, to an outward serenity and an inward peace.

13 Of Miranda I had always thought as an example, that the restraints upon the sex were insuperable only to those who think them so, or who noisily strive to break them. She had taken a course of her own, and no man stood in her way. Many of her acts had been unusual, but excited no uproar. Few helped, but none checked her; and the many men who knew her mind and her life, showed to her confidence as to a brother, gentleness as to a sister. And not only refined, but very coarse men approved and aided one in whom they saw resolution and clearness of design. Her mind was often the leading one, always effective.

WRITE

LITERARY ANALYSIS: Margaret Fuller and the Women's Suffrage cartoons included in the text use critical lenses to evaluate society's treatment of women. In a short written response, select one cartoon and compare and contrast the cartoon and Fuller's messages about the role of women in society. Develop your writing with details from both texts.

Declaration of Sentiments by the Seneca Falls Convention

ARGUMENTATIVE TEXT
Seneca Falls Convention
1848

Introduction

The Declaration of Sentiments was signed in 1848 at the first women's rights convention, in Seneca Falls, New York. Its principal author was Elizabeth Cady Stanton (1815–1902), who modeled the document after the Declaration of Independence. Despite its familiar format, the provocative language of Stanton's declaration startled many who read it, including her husband, who reportedly told Elizabeth that he would leave town if she read the words aloud at the convention. She did it anyway. After Frederick Douglass stood and spoke in support, 68 women and 32 men signed the historic document.

"He has endeavored, in every way that he could, to destroy her confidence in her own powers . . ."

NOTES

1 When, in the course of human events, it becomes necessary for one portion of the family of man to assume among the people of the earth a position different from that which they have hitherto occupied, but one to which the laws of nature and of nature's God entitle them, a decent respect to the opinions of mankind requires that they should declare the causes that impel them to such a course.

2 We hold these truths to be self-evident: that all men and women are created equal; that they are endowed by their Creator with certain inalienable rights; that among these are life, liberty, and the pursuit of happiness; that to secure these rights governments are instituted, deriving their just powers from the consent of the governed. Whenever any form of government becomes destructive of these ends, it is the right of those who suffer from it to refuse allegiance to it, and to insist upon the institution of a new government, laying its foundation on such principles, and organizing its powers in such form, as to them shall seem most likely to effect their safety and happiness. Prudence, indeed, will dictate that governments long established should not be changed for light and transient causes; and accordingly all experience hath shown that mankind are more disposed to suffer while evils are sufferable, than to right themselves by abolishing the forms to which they are accustomed. But when a long train of abuses and usurpations, pursuing **invariably** the same object, evinces a design to reduce them under absolute despotism, it is their duty to throw off such government, and to provide new guards for their future security. Such has been the patient sufferance of the women under this government, and such is now the necessity which constrains them to demand the equal station to which they are entitled. The history of mankind is a history of repeated injuries and usurpations on the part of man toward woman, having in direct object the establishment of an absolute tyranny over her. To prove this, let facts be submitted to a candid world.

3 He has never permitted her to exercise her inalienable right to the elective franchise.

4 He has **compelled** her to submit to laws, in the formation of which she had no voice.

NOTES

5 He has withheld from her rights which are given to the most ignorant and degraded men—both natives and foreigners.

6 Having deprived her of this first right of a citizen, the elective franchise, thereby leaving her without representation in the halls of legislation, he has oppressed her on all sides.

7 He has made her, if married, in the eye of the law, civilly dead.

8 He has taken from her all right in property, even to the wages she earns.

9 He has made her, morally, an irresponsible being, as she can commit many crimes with impunity, provided they be done in the presence of her husband. In the covenant of marriage, she is compelled to promise obedience to her husband, he becoming, to all intents and purposes, her master—the law giving him power to deprive her of her liberty, and to administer **chastisement**.

10 He has so framed the laws of divorce, as to what shall be the proper causes, and in case of separation, to whom the guardianship of the children shall be given, as to be wholly regardless of the happiness of women—the law, in all cases, going upon a false supposition of the supremacy of man, and giving all power into his hands.

11 After depriving her of all rights as a married woman, if single, and the owner of property, he has taxed her to support a government which recognizes her only when her property can be made profitable to it.

12 He has monopolized nearly all the profitable employments, and from those she is permitted to follow, she receives but a scanty remuneration. He closes against her all the avenues to wealth and distinction which he considers most honorable to himself. As a teacher of theology, medicine, or law, she is not known.

13 He has denied her the facilities for obtaining a thorough education, all colleges being closed against her.

14 He allows her in church, as well as state, but a **subordinate** position, claiming apostolic authority for her exclusion from the ministry, and, with some exceptions, from any public participation in the affairs of the church.

15 He has created a false public sentiment by giving to the world a different code of morals for men and women, by which moral delinquencies which exclude women from society are not only tolerated, but deemed of little account in man.

NOTES

16 He has usurped the prerogative of Jehovah[1] himself, claiming it as his right to assign for her a sphere of action, when that belongs to her conscience and to her God.

17 He has endeavored, in every way that he could, to destroy her confidence in her own powers, to lessen her self-respect, and to make her willing to lead a dependent and **abject** life.

18 Now, in view of this entire disfranchisement of one-half the people of this country, their social and religious degradation—in view of the unjust laws above mentioned, and because women do feel themselves aggrieved, oppressed, and fraudulently deprived of their most sacred rights, we insist that they have immediate admission to all the rights and privileges which belong to them as citizens of the United States.

1. **Jehovah** a form of the Hebrew name of God used in some translations of the Bible

WRITE

ARGUMENTATIVE: During its time, the Declaration of Sentiments by the Seneca Falls Convention created significant controversy. Only 100 out of the 300 attendees at the convention signed the document, and some were concerned that it would cause the movement to lose public support. What made it so controversial? Write a response in which you argue how its rhetoric may have contributed to the controversy. Cite evidence from the text to support your response.

Letter from Chief John Ross

INFORMATIONAL TEXT
John Ross
1835

Introduction

studysync tv

John Ross (1790–1866) was a man of mixed racial identity who became Principal Chief of the Cherokee Nation, whose territory was in present-day Georgia. He wrote this letter to the United States Senate and House of Representatives on September 28, 1836. At that time, the president was Andrew Jackson, who was committed to moving Native Americans west of the Mississippi so that whites could have their land. The Georgia government had harassed the Cherokee in many ways—seizing their land, suppressing their newspapers, dissolving their government, and even jailing white missionaries who were sympathetic to them. Ross's letter is in response to the Treaty of New Echota, made between the U.S. government and a small group of Cherokee. This treaty gave the Cherokee five million dollars in exchange for their moving to Northeast Oklahoma. Eventually they were forced to move; the cruel march west killed 4,000 and became known as the Trail of Tears.

"We are deprived of membership in the human family!"

NOTES

Chief John Ross

1 It is well known that for a number of years past we have been harassed by a series of vexations, which it is deemed unnecessary to recite in detail, but the evidence of which our delegation will be prepared to furnish. With a view to bringing our troubles to a close, a delegation was appointed on the 23rd of October, 1835, by the General Council of the nation[1], clothed with full powers to enter into arrangements with the Government of the United States, for the final adjustment of all our existing difficulties. The delegation failing to **effect** an arrangement with the United States commissioner, then in the nation, proceeded, agreeably to their instructions in that case, to Washington City, for the purpose of negotiating a treaty with the authorities of the United States.

2 After the departure of the Delegation, a contract was made by the Rev. John F. Schermerhorn, and certain individual Cherokees, purporting to be a "treaty, concluded at New Echota, in the State of Georgia, on the 29th day of December, 1835, by General William Carroll and John F. Schermerhorn, commissioners on the part of the United States, and the chiefs, headmen, and people of the Cherokee tribes of Indians." A spurious Delegation, in violation of a special injunction of the general council of the nation, proceeded to Washington City with this pretended treaty, and by false and fraudulent representations **supplanted** in the favor of the Government the legal and accredited Delegation of the Cherokee people[2], and obtained for this instrument, after making important alterations in its provisions, the recognition of the United States Government. And now it is presented to us as a treaty, ratified by the Senate, and approved by the President [Andrew Jackson], and our acquiescence in its requirements demanded, under the sanction of the

1. **General Council of the nation** a governing body for Native American peoples
2. **Delegation of the Cherokee people** a selection of people tasked with defending the rights of the Cherokee people against the U.S. Supreme Court

NOTES

displeasure of the United States, and the threat of **summary** compulsion, in case of refusal. It comes to us, not through our legitimate authorities, the known and usual medium of communication between the Government of the United States and our nation, but through the agency of a complication of powers, civil and military.

3 By the stipulations of this instrument, we are despoiled of our private possessions, the indefeasible property of individuals. We are stripped of every attribute of freedom and eligibility for legal self-defence. Our property may be plundered before our eyes; violence may be committed on our persons; even our lives may be taken away, and there is none to regard our complaints. We are denationalized; we are disfranchised. We are deprived of membership in the human family! We have neither land nor home, nor resting place that can be called our own. And this is effected by the provisions of a **compact** which assumes the venerated, the sacred appellation of treaty.

4 We are overwhelmed! Our hearts are sickened, our utterance is paralyzed, when we reflect on the condition in which we are placed, by the audacious practices of unprincipled men, who have managed their stratagems with so much dexterity as to impose on the Government of the United States, in the face of our earnest, solemn, and reiterated protestations.

5 The instrument in question is not the act of our Nation; we are not parties to its covenants; it has not received the sanction of our people. The makers of it sustain no office nor appointment in our Nation, under the designation of Chiefs, Head men, or any other title, by which they hold, or could acquire, authority to assume the reins of Government, and to make bargain and sale of our rights, our possessions, and our common country. And we are constrained solemnly to declare, that we cannot but contemplate the enforcement of the stipulations of this instrument on us, against our consent, as an act of injustice and oppression, which, we are well persuaded, can never knowingly be countenanced by the Government and people of the United States; nor can we believe it to be the design of these honorable and high minded individuals, who stand at the head of the Govt., to **bind** a whole Nation, by the acts of a few unauthorized individuals. And, therefore, we, the parties to be affected by the result, appeal with confidence to the justice, the magnanimity, the compassion, of your honorable bodies, against the enforcement, on us, of the provisions of a compact, in the formation of which we have had no agency.

WRITE

CORRESPONDENCE: Think about a topic of debate in your local community and write a letter to a local official to communicate your position on the matter. How does the issue affect you, your neighbors, family, or friends? Will it alter an aspect of the area that is important to you? Consider your audience as you compose your letter. How can you most effectively appeal to the addressee? Use language that shows your knowledge of your area and the issue at hand, as well as a style that conveys your seriousness.

A Plea for the Opressed

ARGUMENTATIVE TEXT

Lucy Stanton

1850

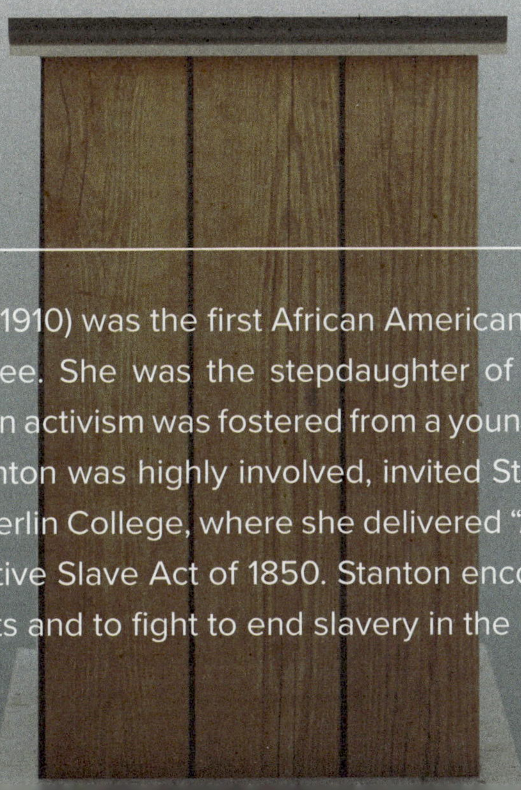

Introduction

Lucy Stanton (1831–1910) was the first African American woman to receive a four-year college degree. She was the stepdaughter of notable abolitionist John Brown, and her own activism was fostered from a young age. The Ladies' Literary Society, with which Stanton was highly involved, invited Stanton to give a speech at her graduation from Oberlin College, where she delivered "A Plea for the Oppressed" in response to the Fugitive Slave Act of 1850. Stanton encouraged others to join the cause of the abolitionists and to fight to end slavery in the United States.

"Slavery is the combination of all crime. It is War."

NOTES

1 When I forget you, oh my people, may my tongue cleave to the roof of my mouth, and may my right hand forget her cunning![1] Dark hover the clouds. The Anti-Slavery pulse beats faintly. The right of suffrage is denied. The colored man is still crushed by the weight of oppression. He may **possess** talents of the highest order, yet for him is no path of fame or distinction opened. He can never hope to attain those privileges while his brethren[2] remain enslaved. Since, therefore, the freedom of the slave and the gaining of our rights, social and political, are inseparably connected, let all the friends of humanity plead for those who may not plead their own cause.

2 Reformers, ye who have labored long to convince man that happiness is found alone in doing good to others, that humanity is a unit, that he who injures one individual wrongs the race;—that to love one's neighbor as one's self is the sum of human virtue—ye that **advocate** the great principles of Temperance, Peace, and Moral Reform will you not raise your voice in behalf of these stricken ones!—will you not plead the cause of the Slave?

3 Slavery is the combination of all crime. It is War.

4 Those who rob their fellow-men of home, of liberty, of education, of life, are really at war against them as though they cleft them down upon the bloody field. It is intemperance; for there is an intoxication when the fierce passions rage in man's breast, more fearful than the madness of the drunkard, which if let loose upon the moral universe would sweep away everything pure and holy, leaving but the wreck of man's nobler nature. Such passions does Slavery foster—yea, they are a part of herself. It is full of pollution. Know you not that to a slave, virtue is a sin counted worthy of death? That many, true to the light within, notwithstanding the attempts to shut out the truth, feeling that a consciousness of purity is dearer than life, have nobly died? Their blood crieth[3] to God, a witness against the oppressor.

---

1. **"may my tongue cleave to the roof of my mouth, and may my right hand forget her cunning!"**: an allusion to the King James Bible, Psalm 137, in which captive Israelites ask God to punish them if they forget their homeland, Jerusalem
2. **brethren** brothers (archaic)
3. **crieth** cries (archaic)

NOTES

5 Statesmen, you who have bent at ambition's shrine, who would leave your names on the page of history, to be venerated by coming generations as among those of the great and good, will you advocate the cause of the down-trodden, remembering that the spirit of liberty is abroad in the land? The precious seed is sown in the heart of the people, and though the fruit does not appear, the germ is there, and the harvest will yet be gathered. Truly is this an age of reform. The world is going on, not indeed keeping pace with the rapid tread of its leaders, but none the less progressing. As the people take a step in one reform, the way is prepared for another. Now while other evils in man's social and political condition are being remedied, think you that Slavery can stand the searching test—an enlightened people's sense of justice? Then speak the truth boldly; fear not loss of property or station. It is a higher honor to embalm your name in the hearts of a grateful people than to contend for the paltry honors of party preferment.[4]

6 Woman, I turn to thee. Is it not thy mission to visit the poor? to shed the tear of sympathy? to relieve the wants of the suffering? Where wilt thou find objects more needing sympathy than among the slaves!

7 Mother, hast thou a precious gem in thy charge, like those that make up the Savior's jewels? Has thy heart, trembling with its unutterable joyousness, bent before the throne of the Giver with the prayer that thy child might be found in his courts? Thou hast seen the dawning of intelligence in its bright eye, and watched with interest the unfolding of its powers. Its gentle, winning ways have doubly endeared it to thee. Death breathes upon the flower, and it is gone. Now thou canst feel for the slave-mother who has bent with the same interest over her child, whose heart is entwined around it even more firmly than thine own around thine, for to her it is the only ray of joy in a dreary world. She returns weary and sick at heart from the labors of the field; the child's beaming smile of welcome half banishes the misery of her lot. Would she not die for it? Ye who know the depths of a mother's love, answer! Hark! Strange footsteps are near her dwelling! The door is thrown rudely open! Her master says—"There is the woman!" She comprehends it all—she is sold! From her trembling lips escape the words—"my child!" She throws herself at the feet of those merciless men, and pleads permission to keep her babe, but in vain. What is she more than any other slave, that she should be permitted this favor? They are separated.

8 Sister, have you ever had a kind and loving brother? How often would he lay aside his book to relieve you from some difficulty? How have you hung upon the words of wisdom that he has uttered? How earnestly have you studied that you might stand his companion—his equal. You saw him suddenly stricken by the destroyer. Oh! How your heart ached!

4. **preferment** promotion

NOTES

9 There was a slave-girl who had a brother kind and noble as your own. He had scarcely any advantages: yet stealthily would he draw an old volume from his pocket, and through the long night would pore over its contents. His soul thirsted for knowledge. He yearned for freedom, but free-soil was far away. That sister might not go, he staid with her. They say that slaves do not feel for or love each other; I fear that there are few brothers with a pale face who would have stood that test. For her he tamed the fire of his eye, toiled for that which profited him not, and labored so industriously that the overseer had no apology for applying the lash to his back. Time passed on: that brother stood in his manhood's prime as tenderly kind and as dearly beloved as ever. That sister was insulted;—the lash was applied to her quivering back; her brother rushed to save her! He tore away the fastenings which bound her to the whipping post, he held her on his arm—she was safe. She looked up, encountered the ferocious gaze of the overseer, heard the report of a pistol, and felt the heart's blood of a brother gushing over her. But we draw the veil.

10 Mother, sister, by thy own deep sorrow of heart; by the **sympathy** of thy woman's nature, plead for the downtrodden of thy own, of every land. Instill the principles of love, of common brotherhood, in the nursery, in the social circle. Let these be the prayer of thy life.

11 Christians, you whose souls are filled with love for your fellow men, whose prayer to the Lord is, "Oh! that I may see thy salvation among the children of men!" Does the battle wax warm? dost thou faint with the **burden** and heat of the day? Yet a little longer; the arm of the Lord is mighty to save those who trust in him. Truth and right must prevail. The bondsman[5] shall go free. Look to the future! Hark! the shout of joy gushes from the heart of earth's freed millions! It rushes upward. The angels on heaven's outward battlements catch the sound on their golden lyres, and send it thrilling through the echoing arches of the upper world. How sweet, how majestic, from those starry isles float those deep inspiring sounds over the ocean of space! Softened and mellowed they reach earth, filing the soul with **harmony**, and breathing of God—of love—and of universal freedom.

5. **bondsman** an enslaved person

WRITE

RESEARCH: Lucy Stanton argues that to achieve peace we must be willing to "plead for the downtrodden of thy own, of every land." Research ways that world leaders or individuals are trying to achieve peace. For example, topics for research may include the efforts of the United Nations, a social media campaign, or a grassroots movement. Write a response in which you explain how the individual or group is trying to achieve peace, using relevant evidence from your research to support your ideas. Explain why their plan is effective and what can be done to make their efforts more impactful.

Second Inaugural Address

ARGUMENTATIVE TEXT

Abraham Lincoln

1865

Introduction

studysync

When newly elected President Abraham Lincoln (1809–1865) gave his first inaugural address, he promised to uphold the Union, even though the issue of slavery had already begun to tear apart the northern and southern states. Four years later, on March 4, 1865, nearing the end of a bitter Civil War, Lincoln stood again on the steps of the Capitol and delivered his second inaugural address. He used this opportunity to reflect upon the war, urge healing, and express hope for the future of the country.

"Fondly do we hope, fervently do we pray, that this mighty scourge of war may speedily pass away."

NOTES

Skill: Primary and Secondary Sources

This is definitely a primary source as it is a historical speech given at Lincoln's second inauguration. He is addressing the nation and immediately points out that the war is still a threat to the nation.

1 Fellow-Countrymen:

Civil War Soldiers Photograph of line of black civil war soldiers holding their rifles circa 1860.

2 At this second appearing to take the oath of the Presidential office there is less occasion for an extended address than there was at the first. Then a statement somewhat in detail of a course to be **pursued** seemed fitting and proper. Now, at the expiration of four years, during which public declarations have been constantly called forth on every point and phase of the great contest which still absorbs the attention and engrosses the energies of the nation, little that is new could be presented. The progress of our arms, upon which all else chiefly depends, is as well known to the public as to myself, and it is, I trust, reasonably satisfactory and encouraging to all. With high hope for the future, no prediction in regard to it is **ventured**.

3 On the occasion corresponding to this four years ago all thoughts were anxiously directed to an impending civil war. All dreaded it, all sought to avert it. While the inaugural address was being delivered from this place, devoted altogether to saving the Union without war, insurgent agents were in the city seeking to destroy it without war—seeking to dissolve the Union and divide effects by negotiation. Both parties deprecated war, but one of them would make war rather than let the nation survive, and the other would accept war rather than let it perish, and the war came.

4 One-eighth of the whole population were colored slaves, not distributed generally over the Union, but localized in the southern part of it. These slaves **constituted** a peculiar and powerful interest. All knew that this interest was somehow the cause of the war. To strengthen, perpetuate, and extend this interest was the object for which the insurgents would rend the Union even

by war, while the Government claimed no right to do more than to restrict the territorial enlargement of it. Neither party expected for the war the magnitude or the duration which it has already **attained**. Neither anticipated that the cause of the conflict might cease with or even before the conflict itself should cease. Each looked for an easier triumph, and a result less fundamental and astounding. Both read the same Bible and pray to the same God, and each invokes His aid against the other. It may seem strange that any men should dare to ask a just God's assistance in wringing their bread from the sweat of other men's faces, but let us judge not, that we be not judged. The prayers of both could not be answered. That of neither has been answered fully. The Almighty has His own purposes. "Woe unto the world because of offenses; for it must needs be that offenses come, but woe to that man by whom the offense cometh." If we shall suppose that American slavery is one of those offenses which, in the providence of God, must needs come, but which, having continued through His appointed time, He now wills to remove, and that He gives to both North and South this terrible war as the woe due to those by whom the offense came, shall we discern therein any departure from those divine attributes which the believers in a living God always ascribe to Him? Fondly do we hope, fervently do we pray, that this mighty **scourge** of war may speedily pass away. Yet, if God wills that it continue until all the wealth piled by the bondsman's[1] two hundred and fifty years of unrequited toil shall be sunk, and until every drop of blood drawn with the lash[2] shall be paid by another drawn with the sword, as was said three thousand years ago, so still it must be said "the judgments of the Lord are true and righteous altogether."

5 With **malice** toward none, with charity for all, with firmness in the right as God gives us to see the right, let us strive on to finish the work we are in, to bind up the nation's wounds, to care for him who shall have borne the battle and for his widow and his orphan, to do all which may achieve and cherish a just and lasting peace among ourselves and with all nations.

NOTES

Skill: Arguments and Claims

Lincoln appeals to both ethos *and* pathos *in order to influence his audience. He describes how both sides pray to the same God yet places criticism on those who ask God to assist in the harm of other Americans.*

1. **bondsman** an enslaved person
2. **the lash** a whip, a means of intimidation or punishment against people who were indentured or enslaved

First Read

Read Lincoln's "Second Inaugural Address." After you read, complete the Think Questions below.

THINK QUESTIONS

1. What do you think was Lincoln's main message in this inaugural address? Cite evidence from the text to support your response.

2. In paragraph 4, the word *interest* appears three times. What does *interest* refer to? Cite evidence from the text to support your response.

3. Lincoln mentions God and the Almighty a great deal toward the end of his speech. Does he believe that God is on the side of the North, the South, both, or neither? Cite evidence from the text to support your response.

4. Keeping in mind that the Latin root -*vent*- means "come," use context from the text to determine the meaning of the word **ventured** as it is used in paragraph 2. Write your definition of *venture* here and explain which clues helped you figure it out.

5. Use context clues to determine the meaning of the word **scourge** as it is used in paragraph 4. Write your definition of *scourge* here and explain which clues helped you figure it out.

Skill: Primary and Secondary Sources

Use the Checklist to analyze Primary and Secondary Sources in Lincoln's "Second Inaugural Address." Refer to the sample student annotations about Primary and Secondary Sources in the text.

••• CHECKLIST FOR PRIMARY AND SECONDARY SOURCES

In order to differentiate between primary and secondary sources, do the following:

- ✓ examine the source, noting the title, author, and date of publication
- ✓ identify the genre of the source
  - Primary sources include letters, diaries, journals, speeches, eyewitness interviews, oral histories, memoirs, and autobiographies.
  - Secondary sources include encyclopedia articles, newspaper and magazine articles, biographies, documentary films, history books, and textbooks.

If the source meets one or more of the following criteria, it is considered a primary source:

- ✓ original, first-hand account of an event or a time period
- ✓ writing that takes place during the event or time period

If the source meets one or more of the following criteria, it is considered a secondary source:

- ✓ a book or an article that analyzes and interprets primary sources
- ✓ a second-hand account of a historical event
- ✓ a book or an article that interprets or analyzes creative work

To analyze seventeenth-, eighteenth-, and nineteenth-century foundational U.S. documents of historical and literary significance, consider the following questions:

- ✓ How is the source reliable and credible?
- ✓ What is the purpose of this source?
- ✓ What historical themes, such as patriotism or heroism, are brought out in the source?
- ✓ How does the author use anecdotes, interviews, allusions, or other rhetorical features?
- ✓ What gives this source literary or historical significance?

Skill: Primary and Secondary Sources

Reread paragraphs 4 and 5 of Lincoln's "Second Inaugural Address." Then, using the Checklist on the previous page, answer the multiple-choice questions below.

YOUR TURN

1. Based on the context in this passage, what can you infer is the historical significance of this speech?

   - O A. It is an example of how to make a strong, persuasive argument.
   - O B. It marks the beginning of the nation's healing and reunification as well as the admission of the sin of slavery.
   - O C. It is a reminder to the Confederate states that they were to blame for the war.
   - O D. It marks the end of the Civil War.

2. In the closing of this speech, the speaker addresses historical themes related to all of the following topics except:

   - O A. war and peace
   - O B. right and wrong
   - O C. the will of God
   - O D. international relations

Skill: Arguments and Claims

Use the Checklist to analyze Arguments and Claims in Lincoln's "Second Inaugural Address." Refer to the sample student annotations about Arguments and Claims in the text.

••• CHECKLIST FOR ARGUMENTS AND CLAIMS

In order to delineate the rhetorical appeals, premises, purposes, and arguments in works of public advocacy, note or do the following:

- ✓ the premise, or the basis of the proposal the individual or group makes, which is often based on logical reasoning and constitutional principles
- ✓ isolate the premise in a work of public advocacy
- ✓ determine whether the premise is based on logical reasoning and constitutional principles
- ✓ identify the purpose of the text and the position the writer takes
- ✓ Identify rhetorical appeals, including appeals to *logos* (logic), *ethos* (trust), and *pathos* (emotions)

To evaluate the rhetorical appeals, premises, purposes, and arguments in works of public advocacy, consider the following questions:

- ✓ What rhetorical appeals does the writer use? What effect do these appeals have on the audience?
- ✓ What position does the writer take?
- ✓ How does the writer use legal reasoning to support his or her position?
- ✓ In a work of public advocacy, how does the individual or group try to influence or support a cause or policy?

Skill: Arguments and Claims

Reread paragraph 4 of Lincoln's "Second Inaugural Address." Then, using the Checklist on the previous page, answer the multiple-choice questions below.

YOUR TURN

1. Which answer best outlines the structure of the argument in paragraph 4?

- ○ A. evidence, reasons, appeals, call to action
- ○ B. historical background, thesis, evidence, appeals, conclusion
- ○ C. conclusion, historical background, and call to action
- ○ D. thesis, background, conclusion, call to action

2. Which sentence contains rhetorical appeals?

- ○ A. "One-eighth of the whole population were colored slaves, not distributed generally over the Union, but localized in the southern part of it."
- ○ B. "These slaves constituted a peculiar and powerful interest."
- ○ C. "To strengthen, perpetuate, and extend this interest was the object for which the insurgents would rend the Union even by war, while the Government claimed no right to do more than to restrict the territorial enlargement of it."
- ○ D. "Neither anticipated that the cause of the conflict might cease with or even before the conflict itself should cease."

Close Read

Reread Lincoln's "Second Inaugural Address." As you reread, complete the Skills Focus questions below. Then use your answers and annotations from the questions to help you complete the Write activity.

SKILLS FOCUS

1. How does Lincoln establish credibility with his audience? What information does he include to prove he is knowledgeable on this subject? Support your answer with evidence from the text.

2. Highlight a passage from paragraph 4 that reveals Lincoln's message. What is Lincoln's claim, or thesis, in his "Second Inaugural Address"?

3. Highlight the passage that contains Lincoln's conclusion. Is his conclusion convincing? Why or why not?

4. To what extent does Lincoln believe that the Civil War was necessary in order to create a more just nation? Support your answer with evidence from the text.

WRITE

RHETORICAL ANALYSIS: In the "Second Inaugural Address," "Letter from Chief John Ross," and "A Plea for the Oppressed," the authors very clearly and powerfully take a side. Select one of the three texts and identify the claim integral to their purpose. Then analyze how the author orders and develops their ideas to support their claim. Evaluate how effective they were in supporting their main argument. Support your response with textual evidence.

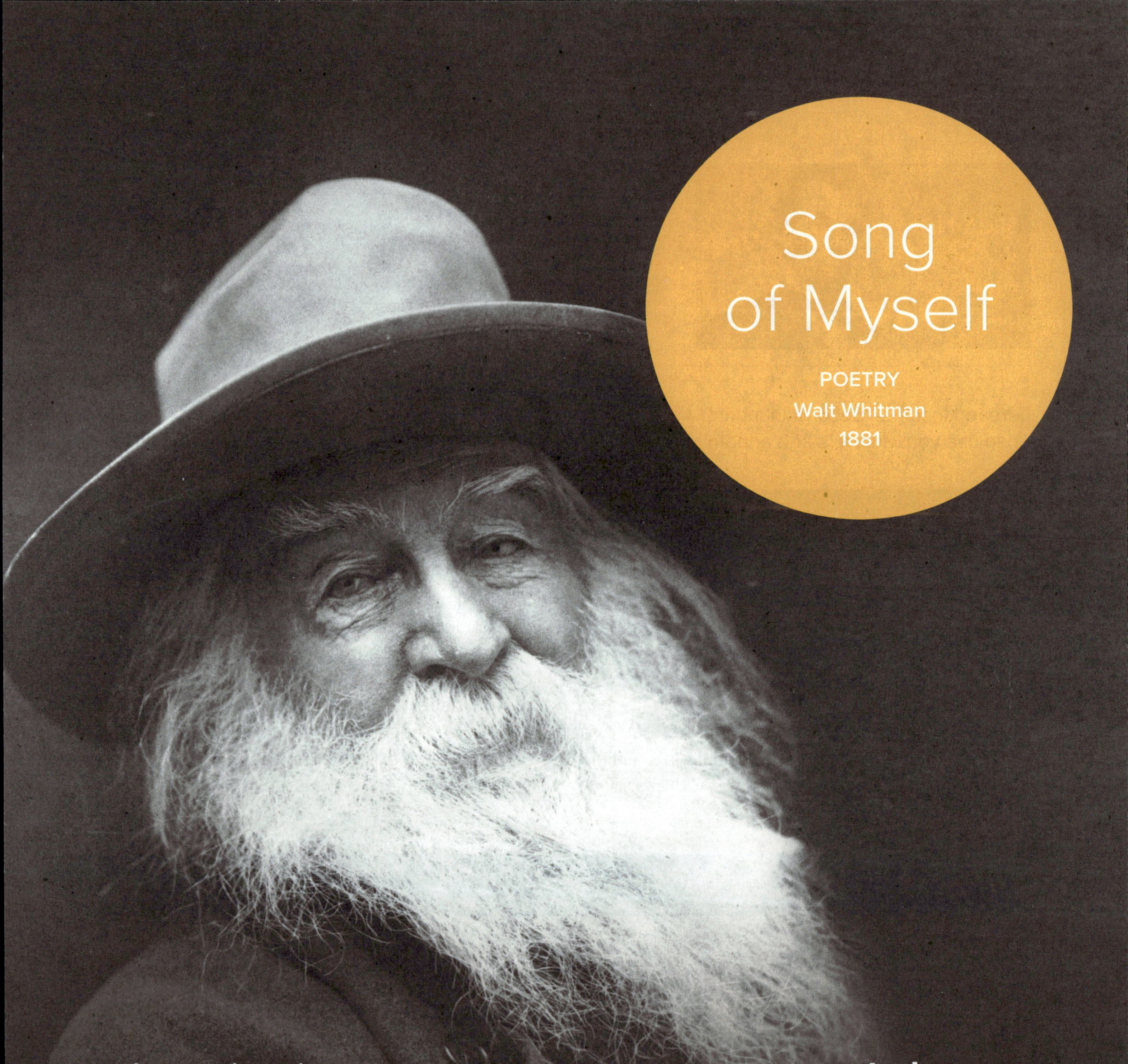

Song of Myself

POETRY

Walt Whitman

1881

Introduction

The opening lines of "Song of Myself" establish the fresh and optimistic tone for this groundbreaking work by Walt Whitman (1819–1892), included in his collection of poems titled *Leaves of Grass*. Often said to represent the core of Whitman's poetic vision, "Song of Myself" was ultimately divided into 52 sections and covers a multitude of topics. In this poem, written in an informal, freewheeling style, with himself as the central character—the *"I"*—Whitman urges the reader to join with him in the celebration of self.

"For every atom belonging to me as good belongs to you."

1

1 I celebrate myself, and sing myself,
2 And what I assume you shall assume,
3 For every atom belonging to me as good belongs to you.

4 I loafe and invite my soul,
5 I lean and loafe at my ease observing a spear of summer grass.

6 My tongue, every atom of my blood, form'd from this soil, this air,
7 Born here of parents born here from parents the same, and their parents the same,
8 I, now thirty-seven years old in perfect health begin,
9 Hoping to cease not till death.

10 Creeds and schools in **abeyance**,
11 Retiring back a while sufficed at what they are, but never forgotten,
12 I harbor for good or bad, I permit to speak at every hazard,
13 Nature without check with original energy.

Walt Whitman

NOTES

Skill: Poetic Elements and Structure

The first line is written in iambic pentameter, but in the second stanza Whitman abandons a set meter. He starts traditionally and then, because he is celebrating "myself," defies any set meter or rhyme scheme.

6

14 A child said, *What is the grass?* fetching it to me with full hands;
15 How could I answer the child? I do not know what it is any more than he.

16 I guess it must be the flag of my **disposition**, out of hopeful green stuff woven.

17 Or I guess it is the handkerchief of the Lord,
18 A scented gift and remembrancer designedly dropt,
19 Bearing the owner's name someway in the corners, that we may see and remark, and say, *Whose?*

NOTES

Or I guess the grass is itself a child, the produced babe of the vegetation.

Or I guess it is a uniform hieroglyphic,
And it means, Sprouting alike in broad zones and narrow zones,
Growing among black folks as among white;
Kanuck, Tuckahoe, Congressman, Cuff, I give them the same, I receive them the same.

And now it seems to me the beautiful uncut hair of graves.

Tenderly will I use you curling grass,
It may be you **transpire** from the breasts of young men,
It may be if I had known them I would have loved them,
It may be you are from old people, or from offspring taken soon out of their mothers' laps,
And here you are the mothers' laps.

This grass is very dark to be from the white heads of old mothers,
Darker than the colorless beards of old men,
Dark to come from under the faint red roofs of mouths.

O I perceive after all so many uttering tongues,
And I perceive they do not come from the roofs of mouths for nothing.

I wish I could translate the hints about the dead young men and women,
And the hints about old men and mothers, and the offspring taken soon out of their laps.

What do you think has become of the young and old men?
And what do you think has become of the women and children?

They are alive and well somewhere,
The smallest sprout shows there is really no death,
And if ever there was it led forward life, and does not wait at the end to arrest it,
And ceas'd the moment life appear'd.

All goes onward and outward, nothing collapses,
And to die is different from what any one supposed, and luckier.

16

I am of old and young, of the foolish as much as the wise,
Regardless of others, ever regardful of others,
Maternal as well as paternal, a child as well as a man,
Stuff'd with the stuff that is coarse and stuff'd with the stuff that is fine,

50 One of the Nation of many nations, the smallest the same and the largest the same,
51 A Southerner soon as a Northerner, a planter nonchalant and hospitable down by the Oconee I live,
52 A Yankee bound my own way ready for trade, my joints the limberest joints on earth and the sternest joints on earth,
53 A Kentuckian, walking the vale of the Elkhorn in my deer-skin leggings, a Louisianian or Georgian,
54 A boatman over lakes or bays or along coasts, a Hoosier, Badger, Buckeye;
55 At home on Kanadian snow-shoes or up in the bush, or with fishermen off Newfoundland,
56 At home in the fleet of ice-boats, sailing with the rest and tacking,
57 At home on the hills of Vermont or in the woods of Maine, or the Texan ranch,
58 Comrade of Californians, comrade of free North-Westerners, (loving their big proportions,)
59 Comrade of raftsmen and coalmen, comrade of all who shake hands and welcome to drink and meat,
60 A learner with the simplest, a teacher of the thoughtfullest,
61 A novice beginning yet experient of **myriads** of seasons,
62 Of every hue and caste am I, of every rank and religion,
63 A farmer, mechanic, artist, gentleman, sailor, quaker,
64 Prisoner, fancy-man, rowdy, lawyer, physician, priest.

65 I resist any thing better than my own diversity,
66 Breathe the air but leave plenty after me,
67 And am not stuck up, and am in my place.

68 (The moth and the fish-eggs are in their place,
69 The bright suns I see and the dark suns I cannot see are in their place,
70 The palpable is in its place and the impalpable is in its place.)

46

71 I know I have the best of time and space, and was never measured and never will be measured.

NOTES

Skill: Poetic Elements and Structure

Whitman uses repetition as a structural element to organize each line. He repeats the words "at home" to emphasize the many different places he feels comfortable, as if he is at one with the whole world.

NOTES

72 I tramp a perpetual journey, (come listen all!)
73 My signs are a rain-proof coat, good shoes, and a staff cut from the woods,
74 No friend of mine takes his ease in my chair,
75 I have no chair, no church, no philosophy,
76 I lead no man to a dinner-table, library, exchange,
77 But each man and each woman of you I lead upon a knoll,
78 My left hand hooking you round the waist,
79 My right hand pointing to landscapes of continents, and the public road.

80 Not I, not any one else, can travel that road for you,
81 You must travel it for yourself.

82 It is not far, it is within reach,
83 Perhaps you have been on it since you were born and did not know,
84 Perhaps it is everywhere on water and on land.

85 Shoulder your duds dear son, and I will mine, and let us hasten forth,
86 Wonderful cities and free nations we shall fetch as we go.

87 If you tire, give me both burdens, and rest the chuff of your hand on my hip,
88 And in due time you shall repay the same service to me,
89 For after we start we never lie by again.

90 This day before dawn I ascended a hill, and look'd at the crowded heaven,
91 And I said to my spirit *When we become the enfolders of those orbs, and the pleasure and knowledge of every thing in them, shall we be fill'd and satisfied then?*
92 And my spirit said *No, we but level that lift to pass and continue beyond.*

93 You are also asking me questions and I hear you,
94 I answer that I cannot answer, you must find out for yourself.

95 Sit a while dear son,
96 Here are biscuits to eat and here is milk to drink,
97 But as soon as you sleep and renew yourself in sweet clothes, I kiss you with a good-by kiss and open the gate for your egress hence.

98 Long enough have you dream'd **contemptible** dreams,
99 Now I wash the gum from your eyes,
100 You must habit yourself to the dazzle of the light and of every moment of your life.

101 Long have you timidly waded holding a plank by the shore,
102 Now I will you to be a bold swimmer,
103 To jump off in the midst of the sea, rise again, nod to me, shout, and laughingly dash with your hair.

NOTES

52

104 The spotted hawk swoops by and accuses me, he complains of my gab and my loitering.

105 I too am not a bit tamed, I too am untranslatable.
106 I sound my barbaric yawp over the roofs of the world.

107 The last scud of day holds back for me,
108 It flings my likeness after the rest and true as any on the shadow'd wilds,
109 It coaxes me to the vapor and the dusk.

110 I depart as air, I shake my white locks at the runaway sun,
111 I effuse my flesh in eddies, and drift it in lacy jags.

112 I bequeath myself to the dirt to grow from the grass I love,
113 If you want me again look for me under your boot-soles.

114 You will hardly know who I am or what I mean,
115 But I shall be good health to you nevertheless,
116 And filter and fibre your blood.

117 Failing to fetch me at first keep encouraged,
118 Missing me one place search another,
119 I stop somewhere waiting for you.

First Read

Read "Song of Myself." After you read, complete the Think Questions below.

THINK QUESTIONS

1. What do you learn about the speaker of the poem? How would you describe the speaker? Cite evidence from the text to support your response.

2. In section 6, how does the image of grass represent the cycle of life and death? Cite evidence from the text to support your response.

3. Many critics believe that Whitman's poetry celebrates the democratic spirit and human equality. What evidence in section 16 do you find to support this interpretation?

4. Use context clues to determine the meaning of **disposition** as it is used in "Song of Myself." Write your definition here, and describe which clues led you to it.

5. How does knowing the root word and suffix of **contemptible** help you understand the word's meaning in line 98? How does the word *contemptible* contrast with what the speaker advises his "son" to do in the same stanza?

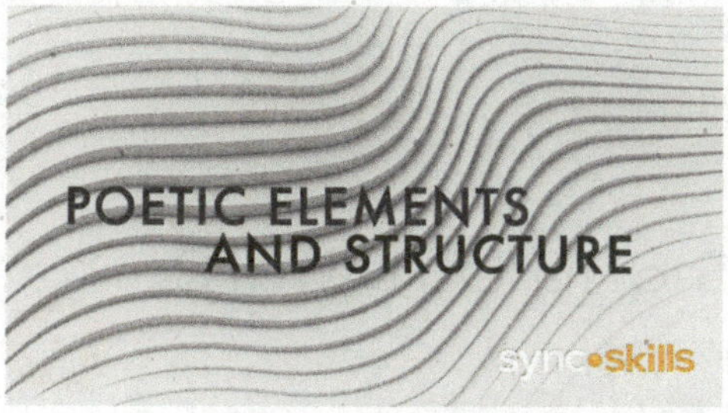

Skill:
Poetic Elements and Structure

Use the Checklist to analyze Poetic Elements and Structure in "Song of Myself." Refer to the sample student annotations about Poetic Elements and Structure in the text.

••• CHECKLIST FOR POETIC ELEMENTS AND STRUCTURE

In order to identify a poet's choices concerning how to structure specific parts of a poem, note the following:

- ✓ the forms and overall structure of the poem
- ✓ the rhyme, rhythm, and meter, if present
- ✓ lines and stanzas in the poem that suggest its meanings and aesthetic impact
- ✓ how the poet began or ended the poem
- ✓ if the poet provided a comedic or tragic resolution

To analyze how an author's choices concerning how to structure specific parts of a text contribute to its overall structure and meaning as well as its aesthetic impact, consider the following questions:

- ✓ How does the poet structure the poem? How does he or she structure specific parts?
- ✓ How do the poet's choices contribute to the poem's overall structure and meaning as well as its aesthetic impact?

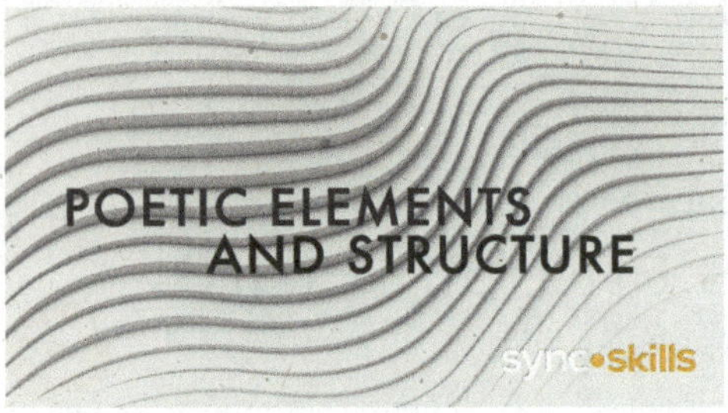

Skill: Poetic Elements and Structure

Reread lines 93–97 of "Song of Myself." Then, using the Checklist on the previous page, answer the multiple-choice questions below.

YOUR TURN

1. This question has two parts. First, answer Part A. Then, answer Part B.

Part A: Based on the poetic structure in lines 93–97, the reader can conclude that—

- ○ A. these stanzas have a regular pattern of rhythm created by the consistent line length.
- ○ B. these stanzas have a pattern of rhythm created by repetition of words and phrases.
- ○ C. the stanzas and lines show this is a formal style of writing.
- ○ D. all of the stanzas have two lines.

Part B: The poetic element that best proves the answer in Part A is that—

- ○ A. the poem becomes difficult to follow without regular numbers of lines per stanza.
- ○ B. the poem lacks coherent meaning due to its overly loose structure.
- ○ C. the poem has a free, loose structure that supports Whitman's fresh, celebratory message.
- ○ D. the poem relies on a rhyme structure to contribute to its meaning instead.

Close Read

Reread "Song of Myself." As you reread, complete the Skills Focus questions below. Then use your answers and annotations from the questions to help you complete the Write activity.

SKILLS FOCUS

1. Identify a stanza or set of stanzas in "Song of Myself" in which the structure or rhyme scheme is particularly interesting. Explain how the author's choices with these lines reflect the theme of the poem.

2. Highlight lines in the last section of "Song of Myself" that show the speaker's beliefs about death. Explain what the speaker's style conveys about his beliefs.

3. Explain how the poem reflects the way the speaker's experiences inform his perspective about self. Use evidence from the text to support your response.

WRITE

LITERARY ANALYSIS: "Song of Myself" conveys a theme about the importance of identity and the expression of "self." Write a response in which you analyze how Walt Whitman uses poetic elements to convey this theme. Support your analysis with evidence from the poem.

A Song for Myself

POETRY
Melvin B. Tolson
1965

Introduction

Melvin B. Tolson (1898–1966) was an African American poet known for his unique style and poetic structure. He was appointed poet laureate of Liberia in 1947, but it wasn't until a year before his death that Tolson published what many consider to be his masterpiece, *Harlem Gallery*, in 1965. "A Song for Myself" is a poem from this beloved collection in which a speaker contemplates the life to come.

"A man
Is what
He saves"

NOTES

I judge
My soul
Eagle
Nor mole:
A man
Is what
He saves
From rot.

The corn
Will fat
A hog
Or rat:
Are these
Dry bones
A hut's
Or throne's?

Who filled
The moat
'Twixt sheep
And goat?[1]
Let Death,
The twin
of Life,
Slip in?

1. **'Twixt sheep/And goat?** This refers to the Christian Bible and the book of Matthew, in which there is a prophecy about God separating his children, the sheep, from those who are not his children, the goats.

NOTES

Prophets
Arise,
Mask-hid,
Unwise,
Divide
The earth
By class
and birth.

Caesars[2]
Without,
The People
Shall **rout**;
Caesars
Within,
Crush flat
As tin.

Who makes
A noose
Envies
The goose.
Who digs
A pit
Dices
For it.

Shall tears
Be shed
For those
Whose bread
Is thieved
Headlong?
Tears right
No wrong.

Prophets
Shall teach
The meek
To reach.
Leave not
To God
The boot
And rod.

2. **Caesars** titles used by Roman emperors

NOTES

The straight
Lines curve?
Failure
Of nerve?
Blind-spots
Assail?
Times have
Their Braille.

If hue
Of skin
Trademark
A sin,
Blame not
The *make*
For God's
Mistake.

Since flesh
And bone
Turn dust
And stone,
With life
So brief,
Why add
To grief?

I sift
The **chaff**
From wheat[3]
and laugh.
No curse
Can stop
The tick
Of clock.

3. **The chaff / From wheat** also referring to the book of Matthew, wherein God separates those who are truly repentant (the desirable "wheat") from those who are not (the undesirable "chaff")

NOTES

Those who
Wall in
Themselves
And grin
Commit
Incest
And spawn
A pest.

What's writ
In vice
Is writ
In ice.
The truth
Is not
Of fruits
That rot.

A sponge,
The mind
Soaks in
The kind
Of stuff
That fate's
Milieu
Dictates.

Jesus,
Mozart,
Shakespeare,
Descartes,
Lenin,
Chladni,
Have lodged
With me.

I snatch
From hooks
The meat
Of books.
I seek
Frontiers,
Not worlds
On **biers**.

NOTES

The snake
Entoils
The pig
With coils.
The pig's
Skewed wail
Does not
Prevail.

Old men
Grow worse
With prayer
Or curse:
Their staffs
Thwack youth
Starved thin
For truth.

Today
The Few
Yield poets
Their due;
Tomorrow
The Mass
Judgment[4]
Shall pass.

I harbor
One fear
If death
Crouch near:
Does my
Creed span
The Gulf
Of Man?

And when
I go
In calm
Or blow
From mice
And men,
Selah!
What . . . then?

4. **The Mass / Judgment** the Final Judgment in the Christian religion, at the end of the world, in which all living and dead souls are to be judged by God

NOTES

WRITE

POETRY: Tolson draws inspiration from the American Romantic poet Walt Whitman to create his own "Song" for himself. Pick a poet or poem, from previous units or your personal reading, and use your choice as inspiration to write a poem with a similar style, tone, or theme.

Adventures of Huckleberry Finn

FICTION
Mark Twain
1885

Introduction

studysync tv

Ernest Hemingway claimed that Mark Twain's *Adventures of Huckleberry Finn* is the one book from which all modern American literature springs. While capturing cultural changes of the times, Mark Twain (1835–1910) weaves a memorable tale as told by the spirited Huck. In Chapter 1, Huck considers settling into a respectable life with the decent Widow Douglas.

"We got six thousand dollars apiece—all gold. It was an awful sight of money when it was piled up."

NOTES

Note: The text you are about to read contains offensive language. Remember to be mindful of the thoughts and feelings of your peers as you read and discuss this text. Please consult your teacher for additional guidance and support.

CHAPTER I

Skill: Language, Style, and Audience

The author's informal language and informal syntax include contractions, slang, simple words, and colloquialisms. The language helps shape Huck's youthful voice and creates a light, carefree style.

Steamboat Race on the Mississippi by Weingartner's Lith

1 You don't know about me without you have read a book by the name of Adventures of Tom Sawyer; but that ain't no matter. That book was made by Mr. Mark Twain, and he told the truth, mainly. There was things which he stretched, but mainly he told the truth. That is nothing. I never seen anybody but lied one time or another, without it was Aunt Polly, or the widow, or maybe Mary. Aunt Polly—Tom's Aunt Polly, she is—and Mary, and the Widow Douglas is all told about in that book, which is mostly a true book, with some stretchers, as I said before.

2 Now the way that the book winds up is this: Tom and me found the money that the robbers hid in the cave, and it made us rich. We got six thousand dollars apiece—all gold. It was an awful sight of money when it was piled up. Well, Judge Thatcher he took it and put it out at interest, and it fetched us a dollar a day apiece all the year round—more than a body could tell what to do with. The Widow Douglas she took me for her son, and allowed she would sivilize me; but it was rough living in the house all the time, considering how **dismal** regular and decent the widow was in all her ways; and so when I couldn't stand it no longer I lit out. I got into my old rags and my sugar-hogshead again, and was free and satisfied. But Tom Sawyer he hunted me up and said he was going to start a band of robbers, and I might join if I would go back to the widow and be respectable. So I went back.

3 The widow she cried over me, and called me a poor lost lamb, and she called me a lot of other names, too, but she never meant no harm by it. She put me in them new clothes again, and I couldn't do nothing but sweat and sweat, and feel all cramped up. Well, then, the old thing **commenced** again. The widow rung a bell for supper, and you had to come to time. When you got to the table you couldn't go right to eating, but you had to wait for the widow to tuck down her head and **grumble** a little over the victuals, though there warn't really anything the matter with them,—that is, nothing only everything was cooked by itself. In a barrel of odds and ends it is different; things get mixed up, and the juice kind of swaps around, and the things go better.

NOTES

4 After supper she got out her book and learned me about Moses and the Bulrushers,[1] and I was in a sweat to find out all about him; but by and by she let it out that Moses had been dead a **considerable** long time; so then I didn't care no more about him, because I don't take no stock in dead people.

Skill: Summarizing

Huck Finn points out the hypocrisy of the widow's ways.

5 Pretty soon I wanted to smoke, and asked the widow to let me. But she wouldn't. She said it was a mean practice and wasn't clean, and I must try to not do it any more. That is just the way with some people. They get down on a thing when they don't know nothing about it. Here she was a-bothering about Moses, which was no kin to her, and no use to anybody, being gone, you see, yet finding a power of fault with me for doing a thing that had some good in it. And she took snuff, too; of course that was all right, because she done it herself.

6 Her sister, Miss Watson, a tolerable slim old maid, with goggles on, had just come to live with her, and took a set at me now with a spelling-book. She worked me middling hard for about an hour, and then the widow made her ease up. I couldn't stood it much longer. Then for an hour it was deadly dull, and I was fidgety. Miss Watson would say, "Don't put your feet up there, Huckleberry;" and "Don't scrunch up like that, Huckleberry—set up straight;" and pretty soon she would say, "Don't gap and stretch like that, Huckleberry—why don't you try to behave?" Then she told me all about the bad place, and I said I wished I was there. She got mad then, but I didn't mean no harm. All I wanted was to go somewheres; all I wanted was a change, I warn't particular. She said it was wicked to say what I said; said she wouldn't say it for the whole world; she was going to live so as to go to the good place. Well, I couldn't see no advantage in going where she was going, so I made up my mind I wouldn't try for it. But I never said so, because it would only make trouble, and wouldn't do no good.

1. **Moses and the Bulrushers** Huck's mispronunciation of *bulrushes*, the river plants among which the baby Moses was found floating in a basket

NOTES

7 Now she had got a start, and she went on and told me all about the good place. She said all a body would have to do there was to go around all day long with a harp and sing, forever and ever. So I didn't think much of it. But I never said so. I asked her if she **reckoned** Tom Sawyer would go there, and she said not by a considerable sight. I was glad about that, because I wanted him and me to be together.

8 Miss Watson she kept pecking at me, and it got tiresome and lonesome. By and by they fetched the n-----s in and had prayers, and then everybody was off to bed. I went up to my room with a piece of candle, and put it on the table. Then I set down in a chair by the window and tried to think of something cheerful, but it warn't no use. I felt so lonesome I most wished I was dead. The stars were shining, and the leaves rustled in the woods ever so mournful; and I heard an owl, away off, who-whooing about somebody that was dead, and a whippowill and a dog crying about somebody that was going to die; and the wind was trying to whisper something to me, and I couldn't make out what it was, and so it made the cold shivers run over me. Then away out in the woods I heard that kind of a sound that a ghost makes when it wants to tell about something that's on its mind and can't make itself understood, and so can't rest easy in its grave, and has to go about that way every night grieving. I got so down-hearted and scared I did wish I had some company. Pretty soon a spider went crawling up my shoulder, and I flipped it off and it lit in the candle; and before I could budge it was all shriveled up. I didn't need anybody to tell me that that was an awful bad sign and would fetch me some bad luck, so I was scared and most shook the clothes off of me. I got up and turned around in my tracks three times and crossed my breast every time; and then I tied up a little lock of my hair with a thread to keep witches away. But I hadn't no confidence. You do that when you've lost a horseshoe that you've found, instead of nailing it up over the door, but I hadn't ever heard anybody say it was any way to keep off bad luck when you'd killed a spider.

9 I set down again, a-shaking all over, and got out my pipe for a smoke; for the house was all as still as death now, and so the widow wouldn't know. Well, after a long time I heard the clock away off in the town go boom—boom—boom—twelve licks; and all still again—stiller than ever. Pretty soon I heard a twig snap down in the dark amongst the trees—something was a stirring. I set still and listened. Directly I could just barely hear a "me-yow! me-yow!" down there. That was good! Says I, "me-yow! me-yow!" as soft as I could, and then I put out the light and **scrambled** out of the window on to the shed. Then I slipped down to the ground and crawled in among the trees, and, sure enough, there was Tom Sawyer waiting for me.

First Read

Read *Adventures of Huckleberry Finn*. After you read, complete the Think Questions below.

THINK QUESTIONS

1. How does Huck describe living with the Widow Douglas? What does Huck's view of the widow reveal about himself? Cite evidence from the text to support your response.

2. What is the conflict between Huck Finn and Miss Watson? How does this conflict reveal that the two characters do not fully understand each other? Cite evidence from the text to support your response.

3. In paragraph 8, how does Huck feel? How does Huck's description of the evening reflect his own mood? Cite evidence from the text to support your response.

4. Read the following dictionary entry:

   reckon
   reck•on \ re' kən \ *verb*

   1. to estimate
   2. to determine based on referencing
   3. to count or calculate
   4. to think or regard

   Decide which definition best matches **reckon** as it is used in *Adventures of Huckleberry Finn*. Write that definition of *reckon* here as well as the clues from the text that helped you determine the meaning.

5. Use context clues to determine the meaning of the word **scrambled**. Write your best definition here, along with the words and phrases that were most helpful in coming to your conclusion. Then, check a dictionary to confirm your understanding.

Skill: Summarizing

Use the Checklist to analyze Summarizing in *Adventures of Huckleberry Finn*. Refer to the sample student annotation about Summarizing in the text.

••• CHECKLIST FOR SUMMARIZING

In order to determine how to write an objective summary of a text, consider the following:

- ✓ find details that answer the basic questions *who, what, where, when, why,* and *how*
- ✓ identify key details that support theme, plot, and other major story elements
- ✓ exclude from summaries minor details that don't contribute to the theme or plot
- ✓ exclude from summaries personal thoughts, judgments, or opinions to ensure that the summaries are objective

To provide an objective summary of a text, consider the following questions:

- ✓ What are the answers to the basic *who, what, where, when, why,* and *how* questions?
- ✓ Have I included major details that support story elements?
- ✓ Have I avoided including minor details that don't contribute to the theme or plot?
- ✓ Is my summary objective, or have I added my own thoughts, judgments, and personal opinions?

Skill: Summarizing

Reread paragraphs 8 and 9 of *Adventures of Huckleberry Finn*. Then, using the Checklist on the previous page, answer the multiple-choice questions below.

YOUR TURN

1. Which statement provides the most objective summary of the information from paragraph 8?

   ○ A. Huck is a coward; he is afraid of everything.
   ○ B. Huck is afraid as he thinks about the darkness and loneliness of the night.
   ○ C. Huck is deeply superstitious, but his fears of darkness and loneliness are real.
   ○ D. Huck has a right to be afraid because the frontier was full of dangers.

2. Which statement provides the most objective summary of the information from paragraph 9?

   ○ A. Late at night, Huck likes to smoke behind the Widow's back.
   ○ B. After midnight, Huck's smoking is interrupted by Tom's meow signal.
   ○ C. Tom Sawyer signals Huck at the Widow Douglas's.
   ○ D. Huck tries to calm himself after the spider scare.

Skill: Language, Style, and Audience

Use the Checklist to analyze Language, Style, and Audience in *Adventures of Huckleberry Finn*. Refer to the sample student annotation about Language, Style, and Audience in the text.

••• CHECKLIST FOR LANGUAGE, STYLE, AND AUDIENCE

In order to determine an author's style and possible intended audience, do the following:

- ✓ identify and define any unfamiliar words or phrases that have multiple meanings
- ✓ identify language that is particularly fresh, engaging, or beautiful
- ✓ analyze the surrounding words and phrases as well as the context in which the specific words are being used
- ✓ determine if syntax is simple or complex, traditional or nontraditional, and its effects on mood, voice, and tone
- ✓ determine style of language and connections to the voice(s) of characters
- ✓ determine audience—both intended and unintended—and possible reactions to the author's word choice and style, considering period of publication
- ✓ examine your reaction to the author's word choice and how the author's choice affected your reaction

To analyze the impact of a specific word choice on meaning, including words with multiple meanings or language that is particularly fresh, engaging, or beautiful, consider the following questions:

- ✓ How does the author's use of vernacular enhance or change what is being described?
- ✓ How does the author's use of vernacular relate to the syntax used in the text?
- ✓ How would a specific phrase or sentence sound different or shift in meaning if standard English were used?
- ✓ How would the text be different if another type of technique or standard English words were used?
- ✓ How does the author's choice of language help reveal a character's tone toward a situation or another character?

Skill: Language, Style, and Audience

Reread paragraph 6 of *Adventures of Huckleberry Finn*. Then, using the Checklist on the previous page, answer the multiple-choice questions below.

YOUR TURN

1. How does the author's use of specific word choices suggest Huck's attitude toward the sister?

   - ○ A. Huck's use of "tolerable" to describe her weight suggests that he accepts her as she is.
   - ○ B. His repetition of "All I wanted" indicates Huck's need for independence.
   - ○ C. Phrases like "old maid" and "deadly dull" suggest that he dislikes her.
   - ○ D. The phrase "never said so" reveals Huck's fear that he cannot meet her expectations.

2. What effect do Miss Watson's repetitious commands to Huck have on the reader?

   - ○ A. Her "Don't" commands create sympathy for Huck.
   - ○ B. They create compassion for Miss Watson, who is tirelessly trying to help Huck.
   - ○ C. The reader understands that Miss Watson is an unhappy person who does not understand children.
   - ○ D. The reader understands Miss Watson's frustration and failure to help Huck.

3. What effect does the author's varied syntax have on the narrator's voice and style?

   - ○ A. It helps create a formal, melancholy voice.
   - ○ B. It helps shape the voice of a likable, well-educated young man.
   - ○ C. It helps shape an uneven voice that is sometimes playful and sometimes defiant.
   - ○ D. It helps create the voice of a young boy who is carefree.

Close Read

Reread *Adventures of Huckleberry Finn*. As you reread, complete the Skills Focus questions below. Then use your answers and annotations from the questions to help you complete the Write activity.

SKILLS FOCUS

1. What details does the author include to help develop the setting of the novel? What influence does the setting have on characters and plot so far?

2. Summarize the tone Huck uses when he speaks to the Widow Douglas. Which word choices suggest this tone, and how?

3. What word choices does the author make towards the end of this chapter to create a specific feeling or mood? Describe this mood.

4. Find an example of syntax that is different from what you would use. How does the author use this syntax to better help the reader understand the characters or tone of the novel?

5. How do Huck's former experiences described at the beginning of this chapter influence his attitude towards living with the widow? Which style of life is he most suited for, and why?

WRITE

LITERARY ANALYSIS: Summarize the main character's tone towards traditional society. Then, analyze how Mark Twain's choices regarding words and syntax help develop the main character's tone towards traditional society. Support your response with textual evidence.

Extended Writing Project and Grammar

Informative Writing Process: Plan

PLAN | DRAFT | REVISE | EDIT AND PUBLISH

Throughout the mid-nineteenth century, the United States' expansionism informed the development of a distinctly American identity. American Romantic and Transcendental literature demonstrated a commitment to individualism and the greater good. However, as writing produced before, during, and after the Civil War reflects, access to individual freedoms was hugely dependent on one's position in society.

WRITING PROMPT

How do our experiences shape our beliefs?

From nonfiction selections in this unit (including research links in the Blasts), select two or three texts that demonstrate the ways in which experiences inform our point of view. Write an informative essay in which you describe the perspective in each text, the experiences that enabled it, and what the writer may have intended to accomplish through the piece. Be sure to include the personal and cultural importance of sharing this point of view and any risks the writer may have been taking. Your informative essay should also include the following:

- an introduction
- a thesis statement
- a clear text structure
- supporting evidence and details
- a conclusion

Writing to Sources

As you gather ideas and information from the texts in the unit, be sure to:

- use evidence from multiple sources.
- avoid overly relying on one source.

Introduction to Informative Writing

Informative writing examines a topic and conveys ideas and information through comparisons, description, and explanation. Strong informative writing includes a main idea or thesis statement supported by evidence, such as definitions, quotations, examples, and facts, that clarifies and supports the main idea. The characteristics of informative writing include:

- an introduction with a clear thesis statement
- evidence and details that support the thesis
- a clear and logical text structure
- a formal style
- a conclusion that wraps up your ideas

In addition to these characteristics, informative writers also carefully craft their work through word choice and an objective point of view. These choices help to shape the tone and overall style of the text. Effective informative essays combine these genre characteristics and craft to engage the reader.

As you continue with this Extended Writing Project, you'll receive more instruction and practice in crafting each of the characteristics of informative writing to create your own informative essay.

Before you get started on your own informative essay, read this essay that one student, Juliana, wrote in response to the writing prompt. As you read the model, highlight and annotate the features of informative writing that Juliana included in her informative essay.

NOTES

STUDENT MODEL

The Quest for Individual Freedom

1 As the Pilgrims demonstrated when they settled in Plymouth to practice their religion freely, Americans have time and again affirmed the commitment it takes to live a life of personal liberty. Whether the goal is the expansion of the nation's boundaries or personal growth, Romantic and Transcendental writers describe a range of transformations. In the texts *Woman in the Nineteenth Century* and *Walden*, Margaret Fuller and Henry David Thoreau published accounts of their own attempts to commit to a life of individual freedom, devoted to the common good. The different ways that they pursue freedom reveal the variety of experiences possible in nineteenth-century America. While both advocate for individuality, Fuller's and Thoreau's experiences leave them with different perspectives on how that must be accomplished.

2 In *Woman in the Nineteenth Century*, Margaret Fuller describes a perspective on life and society that embodies Transcendentalist values of optimism, liberty, and self-determination. Yet, as a woman during that time period, Fuller finds her attempts to exercise personal freedom limited by the attitudes and beliefs that others hold about women. These societal barriers led to Fuller's strong beliefs about the necessity of women representing their own voices. Capturing these arguments in her writing, Fuller describes how many people believe that women do not need to vote or represent themselves in government. Women already have representatives, they argue, as, "all men are privately influenced by women." This thinking suggests that as each woman has a man in her life, he can effectively act on her behalf in all public matters. Fuller believes that this type of representation is problematic. She argues that many people hold deep-seated ideas about the inferiority of women, clinging firmly to "the belief that Woman was made *for Man*." Men, therefore, can never represent women fairly or with justice since women belong to men. Instead, women must be freed from the supervision and

NOTES

management of men. In making such an argument, Fuller hopes to convey the value of each individual and become an equal part of America's developing society.

3 Fuller's experiences of being barred from the ballot box strengthen her perspective that women can positively benefit society. She suggests that if women were allowed to participate as equally as men "the divine energy would pervade nature to a degree unknown in the history of former ages, and that no discordant collision, but a ravishing harmony of the spheres, would ensue." To illustrate her perspective on the benefits of women participating more equally in society, Fuller describes a woman named Miranda. Miranda's father believed in the equality between men and women. She was the oldest child in the family and was raised "not as a plaything, but as a living mind." Miranda was expected to show all of the virtues of men, such as good judgment and courage. As an adult, Miranda was able to take her place in the world. She made many friends and was able to live freely. Because Miranda did not have to confront negative attitudes about women's roles, Fuller notes that Miranda was able to shape her life according to her wishes and overcome challenges with peace.

4 Another writer of the period who argued for the importance of freedoms was Henry David Thoreau. In his book *Walden*, Thoreau discusses how he participated in an experiment that allowed him to put Transcendentalist values into practice. At the age of twenty-seven, he built a cabin at Walden Pond near Concord, Massachusetts. He lived there for over two years, fully immersing himself in the natural world to escape the forces of society that prevented him from living a self-directed life. The experiment at Walden Pond was formative: Thoreau found his perspective on individual freedom forever changed as a result of his time in nature.

5 Although Thoreau was able to vote and engage in public life, he faced other limitations to his individual freedom. Industrialization had many positive effects, such as more efficient transportation, yet Thoreau found its promises of an improved quality of life unfulfilled. Thoreau uses his book *Walden* to dispute the idea that rapid growth allows for expanded personal liberty. Thoreau suggests that life has begun to move at a faster pace than ever before. As a result, this frantic pace leads people to live hectic lives constantly filled with

NOTES

unimportant interests and pursuits instead of living for themselves. He famously states, "I went to the woods because I wished to live deliberately, to front only the essential facts of life." In other words, Thoreau argues that a life that is away from the constant pressures of civilization allows him to engage more deeply with what he believes is essential.

6 Thoreau's experience at Walden Pond was not just a personal adventure; it also shaped his perspective on the new obsession with building capital. Thoreau criticizes people's preoccupation with money, suggesting that the nation was so concerned with accruing wealth that people were no longer invested in internally bettering themselves. To emphasize this point, he asks, "Why should we live with such hurry and waste of life? We are determined to be starved before we are hungry." Here he uses a metaphor of hunger to demonstrate that people had become so entrenched in producing and consuming things that they were no longer in touch with what they actually wanted as individuals. Thoreau does not believe financial success is a sign of progress or freedom. Because he lived a satisfactory life alone in the woods, he believes that others can find personal freedom in the same manner—a Transcendentalist life of individual liberty is possible simply by emulating his minimalist and nature-based lifestyle. Living these ideals himself likely helped to hone his perspective and gave him the conviction that such a lifestyle was also possible for others.

7 Both Margaret Fuller and Henry David Thoreau desired to prove much about personal freedom, yet they faced very different challenges due to their position in society. Fuller, having experienced firsthand the discrimination that women faced in the nineteenth century, sought to convince others to see the basic potential that each woman has and to allow women to take a more active role in governance. Thoreau spent two years alone in the woods and through that experience created a work that railed against the country's infatuation with building capital. At the core, both writers advocated for individual freedoms. Due to their experiences, however, they held very different perspectives on how that might be accomplished. Whether through the ballot box or an escape from societal pressures, both writers sought to live out Transcendentalist values. Their efforts shaped American perspectives for generations to come.

WRITE

Writers often take notes about their ideas before they sit down to write. Think about what you've learned so far about informative writing to help you begin prewriting.

- **Purpose:** What texts do you want to write about? How do the texts connect to each other and demonstrate how experiences inform our perspectives?
- **Audience:** Who is your audience and what is their connection to the topic of your essay? How will you engage them in your point of view?
- **Introduction:** How will you clearly introduce the topic and the thesis of your essay? What language can you use that is both precise and intriguing?
- **Thesis Statement:** What is your unique claim or observation about the texts? Why is your opinion relevant and significant?
- **Text Structure:** What strategies will you use to organize your response to the prompt? How can you ensure that the progression of ideas is logical and well developed?
- **Supporting Evidence and Details:** What textual evidence might you use to add substance to your essay? Where did you find this information? Which details are essential and which details can you leave out?
- **Conclusion:** How does the information in the body of your essay relate to your thesis? How can you connect the ideas presented in your essay to a greater concept or to society in a thoughtful way?

Response Instructions

Use the questions in the bulleted list to **write a one-paragraph summary**. Your summary should describe what you will explain in your essay.

Don't worry about including all of the details now; focus only on the most essential and important elements. You will refer back to this short summary as you continue through the steps of the writing process.

Skill: Organizing Informative Writing

••• CHECKLIST FOR ORGANIZING INFORMATIVE WRITING

As you begin to organize your writing for your informative essay, use the following questions as a guide:

- What is a brief summary of my topic?
- How can I organize my ideas so that each new element builds on previous material?
- Can I use visual elements such as headings, graphics, or multimedia?

Here are steps you can use to organize complex ideas, concepts, and information so that each new element builds on that which precedes it to create a unified whole:

- definitions
  - > first, define a subject or concept
  - > second, define the qualities of the subject or concept
  - > third, provide examples, focusing on showing different aspects of the subject or concept
- classifications
  - > first, identify the main idea or topic
  - > second, divide the main idea or topic into categories, focusing on how you want to explain your ideas
  - > third, use the categories to provide descriptive details and deepen understanding
- comparisons
  - > first, identify two texts about similar topics to compare
  - > second, identify the similarities and differences between the texts
  - > third, determine how those comparisons reveal larger ideas about the topic of the texts
- cause and effect
  - > first, determine what happened in a text, including the order of events
  - > second, identify the reasons that something happened
  - > third, connect what happened and the reasons for it to the main idea or claim

YOUR TURN

Read each sentence from an informative essay below. Then, complete the chart by writing the organizational structure that would be most appropriate for the purpose, topic, and context of the informative text, as well as its audience.

Organizational Structure Options			
comparisons	cause and effect	definitions	classifications

Informative Essay Sentence	Organizational Structure
Understanding the idea of democracy begins with understanding the meaning of the word.	
The second category of caffeinated beverages that were popular in ancient civilizations is tea.	
Not everyone thinks it is a wise decision to buy a home.	
Every fall, monarch butterflies migrate south to Southern California and Mexico to escape the cold weather.	

YOUR TURN

Complete the chart below by writing a short summary of what you will focus on in each paragraph of your essay.

Outline	Summary
Introduction	
Body Paragraph 1	
Body Paragraph 2	
Body Paragraph 3	
Conclusion	

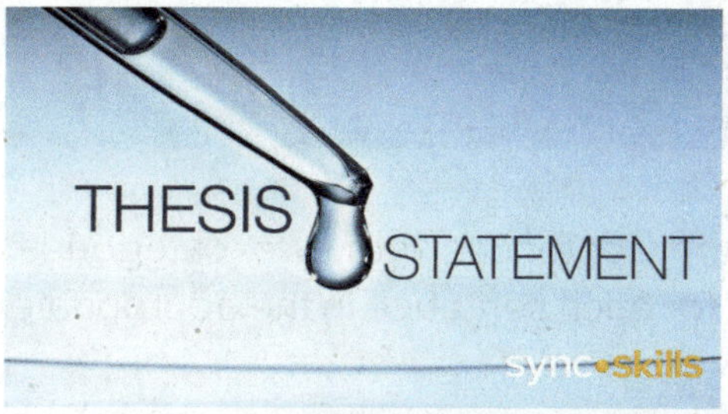

Skill: Thesis Statement

••• CHECKLIST FOR THESIS STATEMENT

Before you begin writing your thesis statement, ask yourself the following questions:

- What is the prompt asking me to write about?
- What claim do I want to make about the topic of this essay?
- Is my claim precise and informative?
- Does my thesis statement introduce the body of my essay?
- Where should I place my thesis statement?

Here are some methods to introduce and develop a topic as well as a precise and informative claim:

- think about your central claim of your essay
    - > identify a clear claim you want to introduce, thinking about:
        - o how closely your claim is related to your topic and how specific it is to your supporting details
        - o how your claim includes necessary information to guide the reader through the topic
    - > identify as many claims as you intend to prove
- your thesis statement should:
    - > let the reader anticipate the content of your essay
    - > help you begin your essay in an organized manner
    - > present your opinion clearly
    - > respond completely to the writing prompt
- consider the best placement for your thesis statement
    - > if your response is short, you may want to get right to the point and present your thesis statement in the first sentence of the essay
    - > if your response is longer (as in a formal essay), you can build up to your thesis statement and place it at the end of your introductory paragraph

YOUR TURN

Read the sentences below. Then, complete the chart by sorting the sentences into two categories: thesis statements and statements of fact. Write the corresponding letter for each sentence in the appropriate column.

Sentence Options	
A	Fuller was unable to vote as a woman in the nineteenth century.
B	Henry David Thoreau's determination to put his own beliefs and abilities to the test proves that people are able to let go of their positions for a more fulfilled life.
C	Margaret Fuller's writing teaches readers that women are equally as capable as men.
D	Fuller's and Thoreau's writings show that social position can limit access to liberty.
E	Although Fuller's and Thoreau's accounts are both about individual freedom, their writings are different because one writer is a man and one is a woman.
F	One of the most fundamental tenets of Transcendentalism is the belief in individual freedom and the greater good.

Thesis Statement	Statement of Fact

WRITE

Use the checklist to draft a thesis statement for your informative essay.

Skill: Supporting Details

••• CHECKLIST FOR SUPPORTING DETAILS

As you look for supporting details to develop your topic, claim, or thesis statement, ask yourself the following questions:

- What is my main idea about this topic?
- What does a reader need to know about the topic in order to understand the main idea?
- What details will support my thesis?
- Is this information necessary to the reader's understanding of the topic?
- Does this information help to develop and refine my main idea?
- Do the supporting details I have support my thesis or claim?

Here are some suggestions for how you can develop your topic:

- review your thesis or claim
- consider what your audience knows about the topic
- note what the audience will need to know to understand the topic
- develop your topic thoroughly and accurately, taking into consideration all of its aspects
- be sure to consult credible sources
- use different types of supporting details, such as:
  - > the most significant and relevant facts that are specific to your topic, make an impact in your discussion, and fully support your thesis or claim
  - > extended definitions to explain difficult concepts, terms, or ideas
  - > concrete details that will add descriptive material about your topic
  - > quotations to directly connect your thesis statement or claim to the text
  - > examples and other information to deepen the audience's knowledge

YOUR TURN

Read the thesis statement and detail options below. Then, complete the chart by sorting the details into two categories: concrete details and not concrete details. Write the corresponding letter for each detail in the appropriate column.

THESIS: In their accounts, both Margaret Fuller and Henry David Thoreau show how experiences can form perspectives.

	Details Options
A	By publishing her ideas, Fuller hoped to convince other people.
B	Fuller suggests that if women were allowed to participate as equally as men "the divine energy would pervade nature to a degree unknown in the history of former ages, and that no discordant collision, but a ravishing harmony of the spheres, would ensue."
C	Both Margaret Fuller and Henry David Thoreau wanted to live a life committed to the common good.
D	Margaret Fuller and Henry David Thoreau published accounts of their own attempts to commit to a life of individual freedom, devoted to the common good.
E	Thoreau uses his book *Walden* to dispute the idea that rapid growth allows for expanded personal liberty.
F	Thoreau's experience at Walden Pond was not just a personal adventure.

Concrete Detail	Not Concrete Detail

WRITE

Use the checklist to create a two-column chart. Write your thesis statement at the top of the chart. Then, in the first column, list supporting details for at least one of the texts you have chosen to discuss in your informative essay. In the second column, list your reasons for including the details.

Informative Writing Process: Draft

PLAN | DRAFT | REVISE | EDIT AND PUBLISH

You have already made progress toward writing your informative essay. Now it is time to draft your informative essay.

WRITE

Use your plan and other responses in your Binder to draft your informative essay. You may also have new ideas as you begin drafting. Feel free to explore those new ideas as you have them. You can also ask yourself these questions to ensure that your writing is **focused**, **organized**, and **supported by details**:

Draft Checklist:

- ☐ **Focused:** Have I made my thesis clear to readers?
- ☐ **Organized:** Does the organizational structure in my essay make sense? Will readers be engaged by the organization and interested in the way I present my information and evidence?
- ☐ **Supported by Details:** Have I included only relevant supporting evidence and nothing extraneous that might confuse my readers?

Here is Juliana's informative essay draft. As you read, notice how Juliana develops her draft to be focused, organized, and supported by details.

STUDENT MODEL: FIRST DRAFT

NOTES

~~Depending on where and when you live, Americans can have a variety of experiences. Margaret Fuller and Henry David Thoreau published accounts of their own attempts to live freely. The authors lived around the same time, yet their accounts reveal the variety of experiences possible nineteenth-century America. While both believe in individuality, Fuller and Thoreau did not agree on how to accomplish this.~~

As the Pilgrims demonstrated when they settled in Plymouth to practice their religion freely, Americans have time and again affirmed the commitment it takes to live a life of personal liberty. Whether the goal is the expansion of the nation's boundaries or personal growth, Romantic and Transcendental writers describe a range of transformations. In the texts *Woman in the Nineteenth Century* and *Walden*, Margaret Fuller and Henry David Thoreau published accounts of their own attempts to commit to a life of individual freedom, devoted to the common good. The different ways that they pursue freedom reveal the variety of experiences possible in nineteenth-century America. While both advocate for individuality, Fuller's and Thoreau's experiences leave them with different perspectives on how that must be accomplished.

Skill: Introductions

Juliana decides to create a more engaging, complex introduction to hook her readers' interest. She provides more context about the history of American liberty and includes inspiring and more descriptive language.

In *Woman in the Nineteenth Century*, Margaret Fuller describes the Transcendentalist life that she would like to live. Fuller finds her attempts to exercise personal freedom limited by the attitudes and beliefs that others hold about women. I would hate that, too. These societal barriers led to Fuller's strong beliefs about the necessity of women standing up for their own voices. She suggests that people expand individual freedoms for women, including the right for women to vote and to represent themselves in government. Some think that this step is unnecessary. Women already have representatives, since "all men are privately influenced by women." People also say that each man has a woman in his life and can act

NOTES

on her behalf in the public realm. Fuller believes that this is silly. She says that many people people hold deep-seated ideas about women, holding firmly to "the belief that Woman was made *for Man*." Men, therefore, can never represent women fairly or with justice since women belong to men. By freeing women from the supervision and management of men, Fuller hopes to show the value of each individual and become part of America's developing society.

Fuller's experiences being barred from the ballot box strengthen her perspective that women can positively benefit society. She suggests that if women were allowed to participate as equally as men that "the divine energy would pervade nature to a degree unknown in the history of former ages, and that no discordant collision, but a ravishing harmony of the spheres, would ensue." To illustrate her perspective on the benefits of women participating more equally in society, Fuller describes a woman named Miranda. Miranda's father believed in the equality between men and women. She was the oldest child in the family and was raised "not as a plaything, but as a living mind." Miranda was expected to show all of the virtues of men, such as good judgment and courage. As an adult, Miranda was able to take her place in the world. She made many friends and was able to live freely. Because Miranda did not have to confront negative attitudes about women's roles, Fuller notes that Miranda was able to shape her life according to her wishes and overcome challenges with peace.

Another writer of the period who argued for the importance of freedoms was Henry David Thoreau. In his book *Walden*, Thoreau discusses how he participated in an experiment that allowed him to put Transcendentalist values into practice. At the age of twenty-seven, he built a cabin at Walden Pond near Concord, Massachusetts. He lived there for over two years, fully immersing himself in the natural world to escape the forces of society that prevented him from living a self-directed life. The experiment at Walden Pond was formative: Thoreau found his perspective on individual freedom forever changed as a result of his time in nature.

~~Thoreau was able to vote and represent himself in public, but face other limitations. Industrialization had many effects, and Thoreau believes this led people to live hectic lives constantly filled with~~

~~unimportant things instead of living for themselves. Thoreau uses his book *Walden* to dispute the idea that rapid growth allows for expanded personal liberty. Thoreau suggests that life has begun to move at a faster pace than ever before. This frantic pace leads people to live hectic lives constantly filled with unimportant things instead of living for themselves. He famously states, "I went to the woods because I wished to live deliberately, to front only the essential facts of life." Thoreau argues that a life that is away from the constant pressures of civilization allows him to engage more deeply with what he believes is essential.~~

Although Thoreau was able to vote and engage in public life, he faced other limitations to his individual freedom. Industrialization had many positive effects, such as more efficient transportation, yet Thoreau found its promises of an improved quality of life unfulfilled. Thoreau uses his book *Walden* to dispute the idea that rapid growth allows for expanded personal liberty. Thoreau suggests that life has begun to move at a faster pace than ever before. As a result, this frantic pace leads people to live hectic lives constantly filled with unimportant interests and pursuits instead of living for themselves. He famously states, "I went to the woods because I wished to live deliberately, to front only the essential facts of life." In other words, Thoreau argues that a life that is away from the constant pressures of civilization allows him to engage more deeply with what he believes is essential.

~~Thoreau's adventure at Walden Pond was not just a personal journey and it also shaped his perspective on the new obsession with owning things. Thoreau criticizes people's preoccupation with money, suggesting that the nation was so concerned with objects that people were no longer invested in internally bettering themselves. To emphasize this point, he asks, "Why should we live with such hurry and waste of life? We are determined to be starved before we are hungry." I think he is saying that people were no longer in touch with their own needs. Thoreau does not believe financial success as a sign of progress. Living these ideals himself likely helped to hone his perspective and gave him the conviction that such a lifestyle was also possible for others.~~

Thoreau's experience at Walden Pond was not just a personal adventure; it also shaped his perspective on the new obsession with

NOTES

Skill: Transitions

Juliana realizes that the relationships between her ideas are not always clear. She reviews a list of transition words and phrases and adds transitions to connect the ideas between paragraphs, emphasize ideas, and summarize concepts.

NOTES

Skill:
Precise Language

Juliana revises her paragraph to make her point more precise. She replaces vague words and phrases such as "things" and "objects" with domain-specific vocabulary, and she adds an interpretation of Thoreau's messages about excess.

building capital. Thoreau criticizes people's preoccupation with money, suggesting that the nation was so concerned with accruing wealth that people were no longer invested in internally bettering themselves. To emphasize this point, he asks, "Why should we live with such hurry and waste of life? We are determined to be starved before we are hungry." Here he uses a metaphor of hunger to demonstrate that people had become so entrenched in producing and consuming things that they were no longer in touch with what they actually wanted as individuals. Thoreau does not believe financial success is a sign of progress or freedom. Because he lived a satisfactory life alone in the woods, he believes that others can find personal freedom in the same manner—a Transcendentalist life of individual liberty is possible simply by emulating his minimalist and nature-based lifestyle. Living these ideals himself likely helped to hone his perspective and gave him the conviction that such a lifestyle was also possible for others.

~~Both Margaret Fuller and Henry David Thoreau desired to prove much about personal freedom, yet they faced very different challenges due to their position in society. Fuller sought to convince others to see the basic potential that each woman has and to allow women to take a more active role in governance. Thoreau railed against the country's infatuation with building capital by spending two years alone in the woods as simply as possible. At the core, both writers advocated for individual freedoms.~~

Skill:
Conclusions

Juliana revises her conclusion by rephrasing her thesis in a thoughtful way and adding a memorable final observation. Her last two sentences reveal the depth of her thinking about both texts.

Both Margaret Fuller and Henry David Thoreau desired to prove much about personal freedom, yet they faced very different challenges due to their position in society. Fuller, having experienced firsthand the discrimination that women faced in the nineteenth century, sought to convince others to see the basic potential that each woman has and to allow women to take a more active role in governance. Thoreau spent two years alone in the woods and through that experience created a work that railed against the country's infatuation with building capital. At the core, both writers advocated for individual freedoms. Due to their experiences, however, they held very different perspectives on how that might be accomplished. Whether through the ballot box or an escape from societal pressures, both writers sought to live out Transcendentalist values. Their efforts shaped American perspectives for generations to come.

Skill: Introductions

••• CHECKLIST FOR INTRODUCTIONS

Before you write your introduction, ask yourself the following questions:

- What is my claim? In addition:
  - > How can I make it more precise and informative?
  - > Have I included why my claim is significant to discuss?
  - > How can I distinguish my claim from alternate or opposing claims?
- Have I organized complex ideas, concepts, and information so that each new element builds on the previous element and creates a unified whole?
- How will I "hook" my reader's interest? I might:
  - > start with an attention-grabbing statement
  - > begin with an intriguing question

Below are two strategies to help you introduce your precise claim and topic clearly in your introduction:

- Peer Discussion
  - > Talk about your topic with a partner, explaining what you already know and your ideas about your topic.
  - > Write notes about the ideas you have discussed and any new questions you may have.
  - > Review your notes, and think about what your claim or controlling idea will be.
  - > Write a possible "hook."
- Freewriting
  - > Freewrite for 10 minutes about your topic. Don't worry about grammar, punctuation, or having fully formed ideas. The point of freewriting is to discover ideas.
  - > Review your notes, and think about what your claim or controlling idea will be.
  - > Write a possible "hook."

YOUR TURN

Choose the best answer to each question.

1. The following introduction is from a previous draft of Juliana's essay. Juliana needs to add a hook to grab her audience's attention and introduce her topic. Which sentence could she add to achieve this goal?

> Margaret Fuller and Henry David Thoreau were both Transcendentalists. These writers engaged with ideas about personal freedom. The means for accomplishing individual liberty were very different. Fuller's and Thoreau's ideas show that your perspective in life is informed by your experiences.

- O A. Have you ever heard of Henry David Thoreau?
- O B. Henry David Thoreau was born in 1817.
- O C. Transcendentalism was a nineteenth-century philosophical movement.
- O D. For good or for bad, people often have very different perspectives on important ideas

2. The following is Juliana's revised introduction. Which of the following sentences is the thesis?

> As the Pilgrims demonstrated when they settled in Plymouth to practice their religion freely, Americans have time and again affirmed the commitment it takes to live a life of personal liberty. Whether the goal is the expansion of the nation's boundaries or personal growth, Romantic and Transcendental writers describe a range of transformations. In the texts *Woman in the Nineteenth Century* and *Walden*, Margaret Fuller and Henry David Thoreau published accounts of their own attempts to commit to a life of individual freedom, devoted to the common good. The different ways that they pursue freedom reveals the variety of experiences possible in nineteenth-century America. While both advocate for individuality, Fuller's and Thoreau's experiences leave them with different perspectives on how that must be accomplished.

- O A. As the Pilgrims demonstrated when they settled in Plymouth to practice their religion freely, Americans have time and again affirmed the commitment it takes to live a life of personal liberty.
- O B. In the texts *Woman in the Nineteenth Century* and *Walden*, Margaret Fuller and Henry David Thoreau published accounts of their own attempts to commit to a life of individual freedeom, devoted to the common good.
- O C. While both advocate for individuality, Fuller's and Thoreau's experiences leave them with different perspectives on how that must be accomplished.
- O D. Whether the goal is the expansion of the nation's boundaries or personal growth, romantic and Transcendental writers describe a range of transformations.

WRITE

Use the checklist to revise the introduction of your informative essay.

Skill: Transitions

••• CHECKLIST FOR TRANSITIONS

Before you revise your current draft to include transitions, think about:

- the key ideas you discuss
- the major sections of your essay
- the organizational structure of your essay
- the relationships between complex ideas and concepts

Next, reread your current draft, and note areas in your essay where:

- the organizational structure is not yet apparent
  > For example, if you are comparing and contrasting two texts, your explanations about how the two texts are similar and different should be clearly stated.
- the relationship between ideas from one paragraph to the next is unclear
  > For example, when you describe a process in sequential order, you should clarify the order of steps using transitional words like *first*, *then*, *next*, and *finally*.
- your ideas do not create cohesion, or a united whole
- your transition and/or syntax is inappropriate

Revise your draft to use appropriate and varied transitions to link the major sections of your essay, create cohesion, and clarify the relationships between complex ideas and concepts, using the following questions as a guide:

- What kind of transitions should I use to make the organizational structure clear to readers?
- Are my transitions linking the major sections of my essay?
- What transitions create cohesion between complex ideas and concepts?
- Are my transitions varied and appropriate?
- Have my transitions clarified the relationships between complex ideas and concepts?

YOUR TURN

Choose the best answer to each question.

1. Below is a section of a previous draft of Juliana's essay. The connection between the ideas in the underlined sentences is unclear. What transition should Juliana add to the beginning of the second sentence to make her writing more coherent and appropriate for the purpose, topic, and context of her essay, as well as for her audience?

> **Not all experiences lead to the same perspective. Henry David Thoreau separates himself from society and lives in a cabin at Walden Pond practice self-determination. This goes to show that there can be more than one way to achieve a particular goal.**

- ○ A. Eventually
- ○ B. For example
- ○ C. On balance
- ○ D. On the other hand

2. Below is a section of a previous draft of Juliana's essay. Juliana did not use an appropriate transition to show the relationship between paragraphs. Which of the following transitions is the best replacement for the word *yet*? Choose the transition that makes her writing more coherent and is the most appropriate for the purpose, topic, and context of her essay, as well as for her audience.

> **Fuller believed that the expansion of individual freedom was the most important thing for people to work toward.**
>
> **Yet, Thoreau spent two years isolated in the woods to achieve individuality. He shunned society in order to truly live a life for the individual.**

- ○ A. Similarly
- ○ B. With attention to
- ○ C. Whereas
- ○ D. As a result

WRITE

Use the questions in the checklist to revise your use of transitions in a section of your informative essay.

Skill: Precise Language

••• CHECKLIST FOR PRECISE LANGUAGE

As you consider precise language, domain-specific vocabulary, and techniques related to a complicated subject or topic, use the following questions as a guide:

- What information am I trying to explain to my audience?
- What domain-specific vocabulary is relevant to my topic?
- Have I determined the complexity of the subject matter and whether any words or domain-specific vocabulary needs additional explanation?
- How can I use techniques such as metaphors, similes, or analogies to help explain difficult concepts?
- Where can I use more precise vocabulary in my explanation?

Here are some suggestions for using precise language, domain-specific vocabulary, and techniques such as metaphor, simile, and analogy to help make complex topics clear:

- determine your topic or area of study
- determine the complexity of the subject matter and whether any words or domain-specific vocabulary needs additional explanation in order to make concepts clear
- replace vague, general, or overused words and phrases with more precise, descriptive, and domain-specific language
- try to use metaphors, similes, or analogies to make information easier to understand
  - > an example of an analogy for a scientific concept is *a cell membrane is similar to the bricks that make up the outside of a building*
  - > a metaphor such as *there is an endless battle between thermodynamics and gravity* can help readers begin to understand the meaning of *thermodynamics*

YOUR TURN

Below is a passage from a previous draft of Juliana's essay. Choose the best answer to each question about using precise language.

(1) Although Thoreau was able to vote and engage in public life, he faced other limitations to his individual freedom. (2) Industrialization had many positive effects, such as more efficient transportation, yet Thoreau found its promises of an improved quality of life unfulfilled. (3) Thoreau uses his book *Walden* to dispute the idea that rapid growth allows for expanded personal liberty. (4) Thoreau suggests that life has begun to move at a faster pace than ever before. (5) As a result, this frantic pace leads people to live hectic lives constantly filled with unimportant things instead of living for themselves. (6) He famously states, "I went to the woods because I wished to live deliberately, to front only the essential facts of life." (7) In other words, Thoreau argues that a life that is away from the constant pressures of civilization allows him to do what matters.

1. Which of the choices would be a more precise phrase to replace *things* in sentence 5?

   - A. nature and camping
   - B. interests and pursuits
   - C. philosophies and religions
   - D. family and the home

2. What would be a more precise replacement for the last phrase in the final sentence in the passage below?

Although Thoreau was able to vote and engage in public life, he faced other limitations to his individual freedom. Industrialization had many positive effects, such as more efficient transportation, yet Thoreau found its promises of an improved quality of life unfulfilled. Thoreau uses his book *Walden* to dispute the idea that rapid growth allows for expanded personal liberty. Thoreau suggests that life has begun to move at a faster pace than ever before. As a result, this frantic pace leads people to live hectic lives constantly filled with unimportant things instead of living for themselves. He famously states, "I went to the woods because I wished to live deliberately, to front only the essential facts of life." In other words, Thoreau argues that a life that is away from the constant pressures of civilization allows him to do what matters.

   - A. allows him to better understand the meaning of life.
   - B. allows him to engage more deeply with what he believes is essential.
   - C. allows him to have some peace.
   - D. allows him to be alone.

WRITE

Choose a portion of your draft where you would like to include more precise language. Use the checklist to revise your draft.

Skill: Conclusions

••• CHECKLIST FOR CONCLUSIONS

Before you write your conclusion, ask yourself the following questions:

- How can I rephrase the thesis or main idea?
- How can I write my conclusion so that it supports and follows from the information I presented?
- How can I communicate the importance of my topic? What information do I need?

Below are two strategies to help you provide a concluding statement or section that follows from and supports the information or explanation presented:

- Peer Discussion
  > After you have written your introduction and body paragraphs, talk with a partner about what you want readers to remember, writing notes about your discussion.

  > Think about how you can articulate, or express, the significance of your topic in the conclusion.

  > Rephrase your main idea to show the depth of your knowledge and support for the information you presented.

  > Write your conclusion.
- Freewriting
  > Freewrite for 10 minutes about what you might include in your conclusion. Don't worry about grammar, punctuation, or having fully formed ideas. The point of freewriting is to discover ideas.

  > Think about how you can articulate, or express, the significance of your topic in the conclusion.

  > Rephrase your main idea to show the depth of your knowledge and support for the information you presented.

  > Write your conclusion.

YOUR TURN

Choose the best answer to each question.

1. The following conclusion is from a previous draft of Juliana's essay. Juliana would like to add a sentence to encourage readers to apply the main idea of the essay to their own lives. Which sentence could she add after the last sentence to achieve this goal?

> Both Margaret Fuller and Henry David Thoreau desired to prove much about personal freedom, yet they faced very different challenges due to their position in society. Fuller, having experienced firsthand the discrimination that women faced in the nineteenth century, sought to convince others to see the basic potential that each woman has and to allow women to take a more active role in governance. Thoreau spent two years alone in the woods and through that experience created a work that railed against the country's infatuation with building capital. At the core, both writers advocated for individual freedoms.

- ○ A. These are both examples of great Americans.
- ○ B. I would like to have a discussion with Margaret Fuller or Henry David Thoreau!
- ○ C. Both people defied society's expectations and sought to fulfill the essential human need to live with personal liberty.
- ○ D. The ideas in this essay can also be applied to other texts.

2. Which sentence in Juliana's final concluding paragraph below best summarizes her thesis?

> Both Margaret Fuller and Henry David Thoreau desired to prove much about personal freedom, yet they faced very different challenges due to their position in society. Fuller, having experienced firsthand the discrimination that women faced in the nineteenth century, sought to convince others to see the basic potential that each woman has and to allow women to take a more active role in governance. Thoreau spent two years alone in the woods and through that experience created a work that railed against the country's infatuation with building capital. At the core, both writers advocated for individual freedoms. Due to their experiences, however, they held very different perspectives on how that might be accomplished. Whether through the ballot box, or an escape from societal pressures, both writers sought to live out Transcendentalist values. Their efforts shaped American perspectives for generations to come.

- ○ A. Both Margaret Fuller and Henry David Thoreau desired to prove much about personal freedom, yet they faced very different challenges due to their position in society.
- ○ B. Fuller, having experienced firsthand the discrimination that women faced in the nineteenth century, sought to convince others to see the basic potential that each woman has and to allow women to take a more active role in governance.
- ○ C. Thoreau spent two years alone in the woods and through that experience created a work that railed against the country's infatuation with building capital.
- ○ D. At the core, both writers advocated for individual freedoms.

WRITE

Use the revision guide to revise the conclusion of your informative essay.

Informative Writing Process: Revise

PLAN | DRAFT | **REVISE** | EDIT AND PUBLISH

You have written a draft of your informative essay. You have also received input from your peers about how to improve it. Now you are going to revise your draft.

REVISION GUIDE

Examine your draft to find areas for revision. Use the guide below to help you review:

Review	Revise	Example
	Clarity	
Identify places in your writing where adding a transition word or phrase will make your writing clearer. Pay close attention to how you transition between explanations and quotations.	Transition into a quotation in the text by adding "He/She states," or "According to [author's name]," before inserting the quotation.	A passionate Naturalist, he aimed to use his own journey at Walden Pond to advocate for a lifestyle grounded by simplisity. He famously states, "I went to the woods because I wished to live deliberately, to front only the essential facts of life."
	Development	
Identify places where your audience may not have background knowledge about your topic. What supporting details could you add to make the content clearer?	Add supporting details to enhance the reader's understanding of words or ideas in your essay.	Thoreau was a prolific writer and prominent figure in the Transcendentalist movement in the nineteenth century. Transcendentalism was an intellectual and religious movement that prioritized self-reliance and the natural world in response to industrialization.

Review	Revise	Example
Organization		
Review your body paragraphs. Are they coherent? Identify and annotate any sentences within and across paragraphs that don't flow in a clear and logical way.	Rewrite the sentences so they appear in a clear and logical order.	He lived there for over two years, fully immersing himself in the natural world to better understand the negative effects of the Industrial Revolution. ~~At the age of 27, he built a cabin at Walden Pond near Concord, Massachussetts.~~ Although industrialization had positive effects, such as more efficient transportation, in *Walden* Thoreau disputes the benefits of the rapid growth of civilization in America ~~even though industrialization had positive effects, such as more efficient transportation~~.
Style: Word Choice		
Identify repetitive words or phrases that do not clearly express your ideas to the reader.	Replace weak and repetitive words and phrases with more descriptive ones that better convey your ideas.	In *Woman in the Nineteenth Century*, Margaret Fuller describes a perspective on life and society that embodies Transcendentalist values of optimism, liberty, and self-determination. Yet, as a woman during that time period, Fuller finds her attempts to ~~live her life~~ exercise personal freedom limited by the attitudes and beliefs that others hold about women.

Review	Revise	Example
	Style: Sentence Fluency	
Read aloud your writing and listen to the way the text sounds. Does it sound choppy? Or does it flow smoothly with rhythm, movement, and emphasis on important details and events?	Rewrite a key passage, making your sentences longer or shorter to achieve a better flow of writing and the effect you want your reader to feel.	These societal barriers led to Fuller's strong beliefs about the necessity of women representing their own voices. Capturing these arguments in her writing, Fuller describes how many people believe that women do not need to vote or represent themselves in government ~~and~~. Women already have representatives, they argue, as "all men are privately influenced by women." This thinking suggests that as each woman has a man in her life, he can effectively act on her behalf in all public matters. Fuller believes that this type of representation is problematic. She argues that many people hold deep-seated ideas about the inferiority of women, clinging firmly to ~~They adhere to~~ "the belief that Woman was made *for Man*." Men, therefore, can never represent women fairly or with justice since women belong to men.

WRITE

Use the guide on the previous page, as well as your peer reviews, to help you evaluate your informative essay to determine areas that should be revised.

Skill: Style

••• CHECKLIST FOR STYLE

First, reread the draft of your informative essay and identify the following:

- slang, colloquialisms, contractions, abbreviations, or a conversational tone
- places where you could use academic language in order to help persuade or inform your readers
- the use of the first person (*I*) or the second person (*you*)
- statements that express judgment or emotion, rather than objective statements that rely on facts and evidence
- places where you could vary sentence structure and length by using compound, complex, and compound-complex sentences
  > for guidance on effective ways of varying syntax, use a style guide
- incorrect uses of the conventions of standard English for grammar, spelling, capitalization, and punctuation

Establish and maintain a formal style in your essay, using the following questions as a guide:

- Have I avoided slang in favor of academic language?
- Did I consistently use a third-person perspective, using third-person pronouns (*he*, *she*, *they*)?
- Have I maintained an objective tone without expressing my own judgments and emotions?
- Have I used varied sentence lengths and different sentence structures? Did I consider using style guides to learn about effective ways of varying syntax?
  > Where should I make some sentences longer by using conjunctions to connect independent clauses, dependent clauses, and phrases?
  > Where should I make some sentences shorter by separating independent clauses?
- Have I followed the conventions of standard English?

YOUR TURN

Choose the best answer to each question.

1. Which type of stylistic error did Juliana make in this sentence from a previous draft?

> **I think naturalism is a very interesting philosophy and it makes Thoreau's journey at Walden Pond all the more powerful.**

- ○ A. The sentence contains an incorrect use of capitalization.
- ○ B. The sentence is too complex.
- ○ C. Juliana uses the pronoun *I* and makes a statement based on her feelings.
- ○ D. Juliana uses slang.

2. How should this sentence be rewritten to address stylistic errors?

> **Thoreau was totally into naturalism, and so he aimed to use his own journey at Walden Pond to get other people really into nature and living a life with less stuff.**

- ○ A. I think Thoreau was a passionate naturalist and he wanted people to live a more simplistic lifestyle.
- ○ B. A passionate naturalist, he aimed to use his own journey at walden pond to advocate for a lifestyle grounded by simplicity.
- ○ C. Thoreau was a naturalist. Being a naturalist was very important to Thoreau. He thought people should live simpler lives.
- ○ D. A passionate naturalist, Thoreau aimed to use his own journey at Walden Pond to advocate for a lifestyle grounded in simplicity.

WRITE

Use the checklist to revise a paragraph of your informative essay to improve the style.

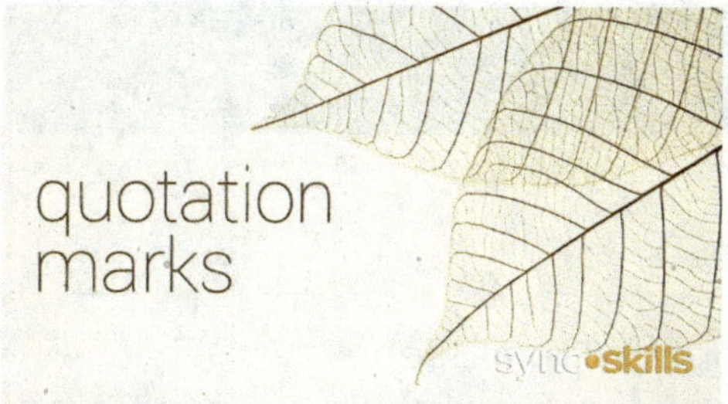

Grammar: Quotation Marks

Quotation marks are used to enclose direct quotations, dialogue, and unusual expressions. They are always used in pairs.

Rule	Text
Use quotation marks before and after a direct quotation or piece of dialogue.	"What do we talk of marks and brands, whether on the bodice of her gown or the flesh of her forehead?" cried another female, the ugliest as well as the most pitiless of these self-constituted judges. The Scarlet Letter
Use quotation marks before and after each part of an interrupted quotation.	"Whenever you feel like criticizing any one," he told me, "just remember that all the people in this world haven't had the advantages that you've had." The Great Gatsby
Use single quotation marks around a quotation within a quotation.	Just before the anniversary, Mr. Tanimoto wrote in a letter to an American some words which expressed this feeling: "What a heartbreaking scene this was the first night! About midnight I landed on the riverbank. So many injured people lied on the ground that I made my way by striding over them. Repeating 'Excuse me,' I forwarded and carried a tub of water with me and gave a cup of water to each one of them." Hiroshima
Do not use quotation marks in an indirect quotation. An indirect quotation is a description of a quotation rather than the quotation itself.	But he bid me tell you, that you might look to unnatural things for the cause of it. The Crucible

YOUR TURN

1. How should this sentence be changed?

   Miss Carson's science cannot be questioned," said oceanographer William Beebe.

   - A. Delete the quotation mark after **questioned**.
   - B. Insert a quotation mark before **Miss**.
   - C. Insert a quotation mark before **science**.
   - D. No change needs to be made to this sentence.

2. How should this sentence be changed?

   Carson's mother taught her daughter that intelligence and personal worth were more valuable than money or success."

   - A. Place a quotation mark after **daughter**.
   - B. Place a quotation mark after **her**.
   - C. Delete the quotation mark after the period.
   - D. No change needs to be made to this sentence.

3. How should these sentences be changed?

   "It was a spring without voices," she wrote. On the mornings that had once throbbed with the dawn chorus of robins, catbirds, doves, jays, wrens, and scores of other bird voices there was now no sound; only silence lay over the fields and woods and marsh."

   - A. Delete the quotation mark after the last period.
   - B. Insert a quotation mark before **On**.
   - C. Delete the quotation mark before **It**.
   - D. No change needs to be made to these sentences.

4. How should this sentence be changed?

   "Did you know that when Rachel Carson wrote her classic *Silent Spring*, *Time* magazine called it "an emotional and inaccurate outburst"?" Simone asked in disbelief.

   - A. Delete the first and last quotation marks.
   - B. Delete the quotation marks around **an emotional and inaccurate outburst.**
   - C. Remove the double quotation marks around **an emotional and inaccurate outburst** and replace them with single quotation marks around the same phrase.
   - D. No change needs to be made to this sentence.

Grammar: Commas with Direct Quotes

Commas separate explanatory text, such as *he said* or *she wrote,* from the words inside quotation marks.

- If the explanatory text comes before the direct quote, the comma follows it.
- If the explanatory text interrupts the direct quote and neither part of the quote is a complete sentence, then the explanatory text is set off with two commas. The first comma follows the final word of the first part of the quote. It stays inside the closing quotation mark. The second comma follows the explanatory text.
- If the explanatory text comes after the direct quote, the comma follows the final word of the quote. It remains inside the closing quotation mark.

Rule	Text
Use a comma between explanatory text and an opening quotation mark.	Lee now looked greatly relieved, and though anything but a demonstrative man, he gave every evidence of his appreciation of this concession, and said, "This will have the best possible effect upon the men." Lee Surrenders to Grant, April 9th, 1865
When the direct quote comes before the explanatory text, use a comma between the final word of the quote and the closing quotation mark.	"Anyhow he gives large parties," said Jordan, changing the subject with an urbane distaste for the concrete. The Great Gatsby
Use a comma both before and after explanatory text if the explanatory text interrupts the direct quote and neither part of the quote is a complete sentence.	"The Montresors," I replied, "were a great and numerous family." The Cask of Amontillado
When explanatory text interrupts a direct quote in which the second part is a complete sentence, end the first part of the quote with a comma inside the closing quotation mark. Put a period after the explanatory text and begin the second part of the quote with a capital letter.	"One of those shot by the carabinieri is from my town," Passini said. "He was a big smart tall boy to be in the granatieri." A Farewell to Arms

YOUR TURN

1. How should this sentence be changed?

> The young Rachel Carson wrote poems and stories, and when a story was accepted by a magazine, she wrote "The pay, I believe, was a cent a word."

- A. Delete the comma after **stories.**
- B. Delete the comma after **magazine.**
- C. Insert a comma after **wrote.**
- D. No change needs to be made to this sentence.

2. How should this sentence be changed?

> John Muir, renowned American explorer and conservationist, said of his school days "We were simply driven point blank against our books like soldiers against an enemy,"

- A. Insert a comma after **days** and place the comma outside the closing quotation mark.
- B. Place a period outside the closing quotation mark.
- C. Insert a comma after **days** and replace the comma after **enemy** with a period.
- D. No change needs to be made to this sentence.

3. How should this sentence be changed?

> "I'll acquaint myself with glaciers and wild gardens," Muir wrote "and get as near the heart of the world as I can."

- A. Insert a comma after **wrote.**
- B. Delete the comma after **gardens.**
- C. Insert a period after **wrote.**
- D. No change needs to be made to this sentence.

4. How should this sentence be changed?

> "Many silent-film stars could not make the transition to sound," Angelo told the class, "because they did not have good speaking voices."

- A. Delete the comma after **sound.**
- B. Move the comma after **sound** to follow the closing quotation mark.
- C. Delete the comma after **class.**
- D. No change needs to be made to this sentence.

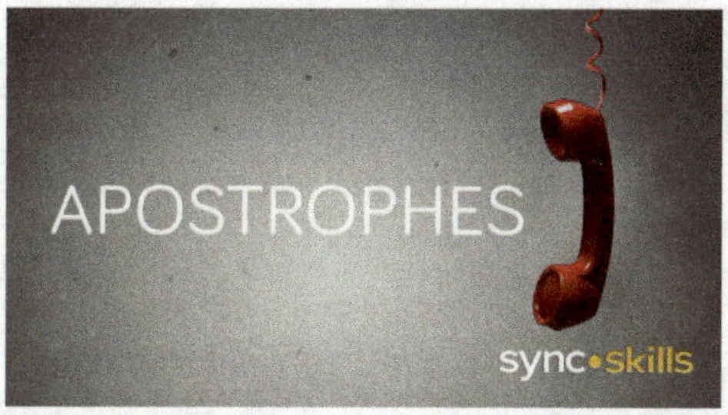

Grammar: Apostrophes

Rule	Text
Use an apostrophe and an *s* to form the possessive of a singular noun.	In the nights in their thousands to dream the dreams of a child'**s** imaginings, worlds rich or fearful such as might offer themselves but never the one to be. The Road
Use an apostrophe and an *s* to form the possessive of a plural noun that does not end in *s*.	These are the times that try men'**s** souls. The Crisis
Use an apostrophe alone to form the possessive of a plural noun that ends in *s*.	I am Dekanawidah and with the Five Nation**s**' Confederate Lords I plant the Tree of Great Peace. The Constitution of the Iroquois Nations
Put only the last word of a compound noun in the possessive form.	The attorney general'**s** schedule was completely full that afternoon.
If two or more people possess something jointly, use the possessive form for the last person named.	All About Pie is the name of Tess and Bev'**s** new pie cafe.
If two or more people possess something individually, put each one's name in the possessive form.	Sarah'**s** and Bobby'**s** SAT scores were excellent.
Use an apostrophe to replace a letter or letters that have been omitted in a contraction.	"I don't know," she insisted, "I just don't think he went there." The Great Gatsby
Use an apostrophe in place of the omitted numerals of a particular year but not with the plural of full dates.	In the 1900s, Soraya was named the homecoming queen of the Class of '39.

YOUR TURN

1. How should this sentence be changed?

> The publisher of Miamis morning newspaper criticized both developers proposed plans for the Everglades.

- ○ A. Insert an apostrophe after the **s** in **Miamis** and **Everglades**.
- ○ B. Delete the **s** in **Miamis** and insert an apostrophe before the **s** in **developers**.
- ○ C. Insert an apostrophe before the **s** in **Miamis** and after the **s** in **developers**.
- ○ D. No change needs to be made to this sentence.

2. How should this sentence be changed?

> Marjory Stoneman Douglas and her friends would visit the Everglades to observe herons nests, spoonbills flights, and egrets at rest.

- ○ A. Add apostrophes before the **s** in **friends** and **egrets**.
- ○ B. Add an apostrophe after the **s** in **herons** and **spoonbills**.
- ○ C. Add an apostrophe and **s** after **Douglas**.
- ○ D. No change needs to be made to this sentence.

3. How should this sentence be changed?

> The Miami newspapers editorial didnt stop the governor from making an assault on the Everglades.

- ○ A. Insert an apostrophe after the **s** in **newspapers** and **Everglades**.
- ○ B. Insert an apostrophe before the **s** in **newspapers** and between the ***n*** and the ***t*** in **didnt**.
- ○ C. Insert an apostrophe before the **s** in **Everglades**.
- ○ D. No change needs to be made to this sentence.

4. How should this sentence be changed?

> Marjory met Ernest Coe, who wanted to protect the Everglades' unique characteristics.

- ○ A. Delete the apostrophe in **Everglades'**.
- ○ B. Insert an apostrophe between the **c** and the **s** at the end of **characteristics**.
- ○ C. Insert an apostrophe after the **s** in **characteristics**.
- ○ D. No change needs to be made to this sentence.

Informative Writing Process: Edit and Publish

PLAN | DRAFT | REVISE | EDIT AND PUBLISH

You have revised your informative essay based on your peer feedback and your own examination.

Now, it is time to edit your informative essay. When you revised, you focused on the content of your essay. You probably looked at how to write an introduction, incorporate transitions, use precise language, and craft a memorable conclusion. When you edit, you focus on the mechanics of your essay, paying close attention to things like grammar and punctuation.

Use the checklist below to guide you as you edit:

☐ Have I followed all the rules for using quotation marks?

☐ Have I used commas with direct quotes correctly throughout the essay?

☐ Have I used apostrophes correctly throughout the essay?

☐ Have I spelled everything correctly?

Notice some edits Juliana has made:

- Added an apostrophe to show possession
- Added quotation marks to a quotation from a text
- Corrected a spelling mistake

Miranda's father believed in the equality between men and women. She was the oldest child in the family and was raised, "not as a plaything, but as a living mind." Miranda was expected to show all of the virtues of men, such as good ~~judgement~~ judgment and courage. As an adult, Miranda was able to take her place in the world. She made many friends and was able to live freely.

WRITE

Use the questions on the previous page, as well as your peer reviews, to help you evaluate your informative essay to determine areas that need editing. Then, edit your essay to correct those errors.

Once you have made all your corrections, you are ready to publish your work. You can distribute your writing to family and friends, hang it on a bulletin board, or post it on your blog. If you publish online, share the link with your family, friends, and classmates.

PHOTO/IMAGE CREDITS:

cover, iStock.com/Vladimir_Timofeev
p. iii, iStock.com/DNY59
p. ix, iStock.com/Vladimir_Timofeev
p. x, Emily Dickinson - Culture Club/Contributor/ Hulton Archive/Getty Images
p. x, Ralph Waldo Emerson - Everett Collection Historical/Alamy Stock Photo
p. x, Margaret Fuller - Chappel PD
p. x, Abraham Lincoln - Bettmann/Contributor/ Bettmann/Getty Images
p. x, Herman Melville - Bettmann/Contributor/ Bettmann Collection/Getty
p. x, Edgar Allan Poe - Universal History Archive/ Contributor/Universal Images Group/Getty Images
p. xi, John Ross - MPI/Stringer/Archive Photos/Getty Images
p. xi, Lucy Stanton - Public Domain
p. xi, Henry David Thoreau - istock.com/wynnter
p. xi, Melvin B. Tolson - Public Domain
p. xi, Mark Twain - istock.com/Grafissimo
p. xi, Walt Whitman - Stock Montage/Contributor/ Getty
p. xii, Cover - ©iStock.com/Ladislav Kubeš
p. 1, Cole, Thomas. The Oxbow (The Connecticut River at Northampton). 1836. Painting. Metropolitan Museum of Art, New York.
p. 4, Getty: Fototeca Storica Nazionale./Contributor/ Hulton Archive
p. 6, Culture Club/Hulton Archive/Getty Images
p. 8, Cover - ©iStock.com/Ladislav Kubeš
p. 9, ©iStock.com/DNY59
p. 10, iStock.com/ivan-96
p. 26, iStock.com/olaser
p. 28, iStock.com/olaser
p. 29, iStock.com/fotogaby
p. 31, iStock.com/fotogaby
p. 32, iStock.com/olaser
p. 33, iStock.com/Nikhil Gangavane
p. 37, coryz/iStock.com
p. 38, Buyenlarge/Hulton Fine Art Collection/Getty Images
p. 41, istock.com/Dirk70
p. 42, FPG/Archive Photos/Getty Images
p. 73, istock.com/Dirk70
p. 74, iStock.com/Dominique_Lavoie
p. 75, iStock.com/Dominique_Lavoie
p. 76, iStock.com/yipengge
p. 77, iStock.com/yipengge
p. 78, iStock.com/fotogaby
p. 79, iStock.com/fotogaby
p. 80, istock.com/Dirk70
p. 81, iStock.com/KateJoanna
p. 83, Public Domain Image
p. 85, Culture Club/Hulton Archive/Getty Images
p. 86, iStock.com/KateJoanna
p. 87, CaseyHillPhoto/iStock.com
p. 89, Rare Book and Special Collections Division, Library of Congress, rbcmil scrp5015401
p. 93, Public Domain image
p. 97, iStock.com/jadimages
p. 98, MPI/Archive Photos/Getty Images
p. 101, Peshkova/iStock/Getty Images Plus
p. 105, Public Domain image
p. 106, Fotosearch/Archive Photos/Getty Images
p. 108, Public Domain image
p. 109, iStock.com/ThomasVogel
p. 110, iStock.com/ThomasVogel
p. 111, iStock.com/DNY59
p. 112, iStock.com/DNY59
p. 113, Public Domain image
p. 114, Getty Archive Photos/Stock Montage/ Contributor
p. 115, Getty Archive Photos/Stock Montage/ Contributor
p. 120, Getty Archive Photos/Stock Montage/ Contributor
p. 121, iStock.com/Andrey_A
p. 122, iStock.com/Andrey_A
p. 123, Getty Archive Photos/Stock Montage/ Contributor
p. 124, istock.com/Martin_Barraud
p. 131, iStock.com/video1
p. 132, Library of Congress/Corbis Historical/Getty Images
p. 135, iStock.com/video1
p. 136, ©iStockphoto.com
p. 137, ©iStockphoto.com
p. 138, iStock.com/antoni_halim
p. 139, iStock.com/antoni_halim
p. 140, iStock.com/video1
p. 141, iStock.com/hanibaram, iStock.com/seb_ra, iStock.com/Martin Barraud
p. 142, iStock.com/Martin Barraud
p. 148, iStock.com/
p. 151, iStock.com/gopixa
p. 153, iStock.com/Tevarak
p. 156, iStock.com/Martin Barraud
p. 161, iStock.com/bo1982
p. 164, iStock.com/Jeff_Hu
p. 166, iStock.com/peepo
p. 169, iStock.com/stevedangers
p. 172, iStock.com/Martin Barraud
p. 175, iStock/Fodor90
p. 177, ©iStock.com/kyoshino
p. 179, iStock.com/wwing
p. 181, iStock.com/BrianAJackson
p. 183, iStock.com/Martin Barraud

studysync

Text Fulfillment Through StudySync

If you are interested in specific titles, please fill out the form below and we will check availability through our partners.

ORDER DETAILS

Date:

TITLE	AUTHOR	Paperback/ Hardcover	Specific Edition *If Applicable*	Quantity

SHIPPING INFORMATION

Contact:

Title:

School/District:

Address Line 1:

Address Line 2:

Zip or Postal Code:

Phone:

Mobile:

Email:

BILLING INFORMATION

☐ *SAME AS SHIPPING*

Contact:

Title:

School/District:

Address Line 1:

Address Line 2:

Zip or Postal Code:

Phone:

Mobile:

Email:

PAYMENT INFORMATION

☐ CREDIT CARD

Name on Card:

Card Number: Expiration Date: Security Code:

☐ PO

Purchase Order Number:

StudySync Text Fulfillment, BookheadEd Learning, LLC
610 Daniel Young Drive | Sonoma, CA 95476